CONTENTS

CLOUD BREAD

Prep: 10 mins - Cook: 20 mins - makes 8 pieces

INGREDIENTS

- oil or butter for greasing
- 4 eggs, separated
- 50g cream cheese
- ¼ tsp cream of tartar
- ½ tsp nigella seeds

DIRECTIONS

STEP 1

Heat oven to 150C/130C fan/gas 2 and line 2 large baking sheets with baking paper, then grease well with butter or oil.

STEP 2

In a large bowl and using electric beaters, whisk the egg whites together until stiff peaks form. You should be able to carefully turn the bowl upside down without it falling out.

STEP 3

In another bowl, put the egg yolks, cream cheese and cream of tartar then whisk together (no need to wash the beaters first) until smooth, pale and frothy. Next, fold the egg whites, a spoonful at a time into the yolk mixture, be as gentle as you can with this so you don't knock out too much of the air and finally fold in the nigella seeds and season with salt and pepper.

STEP 4

Carefully dollop the mixture onto the prepared baking sheets, if the mixture is a little runny when you get to the bottom of the bowl don't use the last few spoonfuls – only use the really fluffy mix on the top. Bake for 20 mins or until lightly golden and craggy on top. Allow to cool for a few moments before carefully removing from the paper with a palette knife.

LOW SUGAR CHOCOLATE SANDWICH CAKE

Prep: 35 mins - Cook: 25 mins - 30 mins - Cuts into 12

INGREDIENTS

For the cake

- 150ml rapeseed oil , plus extra for greasing

- 250g cooked beetroot
- 50g cocoa
- 140g plain wholewheat flour
- 100g plain white flour
- 50g ground almonds
- 200g xylitol , such as Total Sweet
- 2 tsp baking powder
- 1 tsp bicarbonate of soda
- 2 large eggs
- 2 tsp vanilla extract
- 50ml skimmed milk

For the chocolate cream

- 150ml pot natural bio-yogurt
- 2 tbsp cocoa
- 100g xylitol such as Total Sweet
- 150ml pot double cream

DIRECTIONS

STEP 1

Heat oven to 160C/140C/gas 3 and grease then line the base of two x 20cm sandwich tins with baking parchment. To start making the chocolate cream stir the yogurt with the cocoa and xylitol until completely blended then set aside while you make the cake. This helps to dissolve the xylitol granules.

STEP 2

To make the cake, first blitz the beetroot in a food processor until it resembles a thick puree. Tip in the cocoa, flours, ground almonds, xylitol, baking powder and soda and pulse briefly to mix the ingredients together.

STEP 3

Now add the eggs, the 150ml rapeseed oil, vanilla extract and milk, and blitz again to make a smooth liquid batter.

STEP 4

Divide the mixture evenly between the tins working quickly, as the baking powder activates once in contact with the liquid ingredients, then bake for 25-30 mins until a skewer poked into the middle of the cake comes out clean. Cool for few mins then remove from the tins and finish cooling on a wire rack. Once cold, carefully strip off the lining paper.

STEP 5

To finish the chocolate cream, whip the double cream until it holds its shape. Stir the cocoa mixture then fold in all but 2 tsp. Spread a third on top of one of the cold sponge cakes, top with the remaining sponge and spread with the rest of the chocolate cream to create a swirly finish. Dot over the reserved cocoa mixture and gently feather in with the end of a teaspoon. The cake will keep in the fridge for a couple of days, but return to room temperature before eating for the best taste and texture.

HAKE & SEAFOOD CATAPLANA

Prep: 15 mins - Cook: 35 mins - Serves 2

INGREDIENTS

- 2 tbsp cold-pressed rapeseed oil
- 1 onion , halved and thinly sliced
- 250g salad potatoes , cut into chunks
- 1 large red pepper , deseeded and chopped
- 1 courgette (200g), thickly sliced
- 2 tomatoes , chopped (150g)
- 2 large garlic cloves , finely grated
- 1 tbsp cider vinegar (optional)
- 2 tsp vegetable bouillon powder
- 2 skinless hake fillets (pack size 240g)
- 150g pack ready-cooked mussels (not in shells)
- 60g peeled prawns
- large handful of parsley , chopped

DIRECTIONS

STEP 1

Heat the oil in a wide non-stick pan with a tight-fitting lid. Fry the onions and potatoes for about 5 mins, or until starting to soften. Add the peppers, courgettes, tomatoes and garlic, then stir in the vinegar, if using, the bouillon and 200ml water. Bring to a simmer, cover and cook for 25 mins, or until the peppers and courgettes are very tender (if your pan doesn't have a tight-fitting lid, wet a sheet of baking parchment and place over the stew before covering – this helps keep in the juices).

STEP 2

Add the hake fillets, mussels and prawns, then cover and cook for 5 mins more, or until the fish flakes easily when tested with a fork. Scatter over the parsley and serve.

SLOW COOKER MUSHROOM RISOTTO

Prep: 30 mins - Cook: 1 hr - Serves 4

INGREDIENTS

- 1 onion, finely chopped
- 1 tsp olive oil
- 250g chestnut mushrooms, sliced
- 1l vegetable stock
- 50g porcini
- 300g wholegrain rice
- small bunch parsley, finely chopped
- grated vegetarian parmesan-style cheese to serve

DIRECTIONS

STEP 1

Heat the slow cooker if necessary. Fry the onion in the oil in a frying pan with a splash of water for 10 minutes or until it is soft but not coloured. Add the mushroom slices and stir them around until they start to soften and release their juices.

STEP 2

Meanwhile pour the stock into a saucepan and add the porcini, bring to a simmer and then leave to soak. Tip the onions and mushrooms into the slow cooker and add the rice, stir it in well. Pour over the stock and porcini leaving any bits of sediment in the saucepan (or pour the mixture through a fine sieve).

STEP 3

Cook on High for 3 hours, stirring halfway. and then check the consistency – the rice should be cooked. If it needs a little more liquid stir in a splash of stock. Stir in the parsley and season. Serve with the parmesan.

GINGER & SOY SEA BASS PARCELS

Prep: 30 mins - Cook: 15 mins - Serves 4

INGREDIENTS

- 100ml shaohsing rice wine or dry sherry
- 100ml light soy sauce
- 1 small bunch of spring onions , finely sliced
- 2 garlic cloves , finely chopped

- thumb-sized piece fresh ginger , finely chopped
- 4 sea bass fillets, scaled (about 100g each)
- 3 pak choi , each quartered
- 1 large carrot , shredded into fine strips
- 2 red chillies , 4 spring onions, and thumb-sized piece ginger, cut into fine strips, to serve

DIRECTIONS

STEP 1

In a jug, mix together the wine or sherry with the soy, spring onions, garlic and ginger, then set aside. Lightly score the skin of each sea bass fillet a couple of times.

STEP 2

Lay a square of foil on your work surface with a square of baking parchment the same size on top. Put 3 pak choi quarters just off centre of the paper and top with a quarter of the shredded carrot followed by a sea bass fillet, skin-side up. Spoon over a quarter of the ginger, onion and garlic mixture (don't add the rice wine and soy mixture yet). Fold over the parcel so it becomes a triangle, then, from left to right, begin to seal it by scrunching the edges together. Continue all the way around until there is just a little hole at the end. Pour a quarter of the soy mix through the hole. Scrunch the remaining bit to seal and place on a baking tray. Repeat until all the fish are wrapped, sauced and sealed. Can be prepared a day ahead and chilled.

STEP 3

Heat oven to 200C/180C fan/gas 6 and cook the fish on the tray for 15 mins. Remove from the oven and divide the parcels between four warmed plates. Let your guests open them up themselves so they get a hit of aromatic steam before they tuck in. Pass around some chilli, spring onion and ginger strips to sprinkle over.

VEGETARIAN BEAN POT WITH HERBY BREADCRUMBS

Prep: 10 mins - Cook: 35 mins - Serves 2

INGREDIENTS

- 1 slice crusty bread
- ½ small pack parsley leaves
- ½ lemon , zested
- 2 tbsp olive oil
- pinch chilli flakes (optional)
- 2 leeks , rinsed and chopped into half-moons
- 2 carrots , thinly sliced

- 2 celery sticks , thinly sliced
- 1 fennel bulb , thinly sliced
- 2 large garlic cloves , chopped
- 1 tbsp tomato purée
- few thyme sprigs
- 150ml white wine
- 400g can cannellini beans , drained

DIRECTIONS

STEP 1

Toast the bread, then tear into pieces and put in a food processor with the parsley, lemon zest, ½ tbsp olive oil, a good pinch of salt and pepper and the chilli flakes, if using. Blitz to breadcrumbs. Set aside.

STEP 2

Heat the remaining oil in a pan and add the leeks, carrots, celery and fennel along with a splash of water and a pinch of salt. Cook over a medium heat for 10 mins until soft, then add the garlic and tomato purée. Cook for 1 min more, then add the thyme and white wine. Leave to bubble for a minute, then add the beans. Fill the can halfway with water and pour into the pot.

STEP 3

Bring the cassoulet to the boil, then turn down the heat and leave to simmer for 15 mins before removing the thyme sprigs. Mash half the beans to thicken the stew. Season to taste, then divide between bowls and top with the herby breadcrumbs to serve.

BANANA & CINNAMON PANCAKES WITH BLUEBERRY COMPOTE

Prep: 10 mins - Cook: 15 mins - Serves 4

INGREDIENTS

- 65g wholemeal flour
- 1 tsp ground cinnamon , plus extra for sprinkling
- 2 egg , plus 2 egg whites
- 100ml whole milk
- 1 small banana , mashed
- ½ tbsp rapeseed oil
- 320g blueberries
- few mint leaves , to serve

DIRECTIONS

STEP 1

Tip the flour and cinnamon into a bowl, then break in the whole eggs, pour in the milk and whisk together until smooth. Stir in the banana. In a separate bowl, whisk the egg whites until light and fluffy, but not completely stiff, then fold into the pancake mix until evenly incorporated.

STEP 2

Heat a small amount of oil in a large non-stick frying pan, then add a quarter of the pancake mix, swirl to cover the base of the pan and cook until set and golden. Carefully turn the pancake over with a palette knife and cook the other side. Transfer to a plate, then carry on with the rest of the batter until you have four.

STEP 3

To make the compote, tip the berries in a non-stick pan and heat gently until the berries just burst but hold their shape. Serve two warm pancakes with half the berries, then scatter with the mint leaves and sprinkle with a little cinnamon. Chill the remaining pancakes and compote and serve the next day. You can reheat them in the microwave or in a pan.

BLACK-EYED BEAN MOLE WITH SALSA

Prep: 15 mins - Cook: 5 mins - 8 mins - Serves 2

INGREDIENTS

For the salsa

- 1 red onion , finely chopped
- 2 large tomatoes , chopped
- 2 tbsp fresh coriander
- ½ lime , zest and juice

For the mole

- 2 tsp rapeseed oil
- 1 red onion , halved and sliced
- 1 garlic clove , finely grated
- 1 tsp ground coriander
- 1 tsp mild chilli powder
- ½ tsp ground cinnamon
- 400g can black-eyed beans in water
- 2 tsp cocoa
- 1 tsp vegetable bouillon
- 1 tbsp tomato purée

DIRECTIONS

STEP 1

Tip all the salsa ingredients into a bowl and stir together.

STEP 2

For the mole, heat the oil in a non-stick pan, add the onion and garlic and fry stirring frequently until softened. Tip in the spices, stir then add the contents of the can of beans with the cocoa, bouillon and tomato purée. Cook, stirring frequently to make quite a thick sauce.

STEP 3

Spoon into shallow bowls, top with the salsa and serve.

SALMON PASTA SALAD WITH LEMON & CAPERS

Prep: 10 mins - Cook: 20 mins - Serves 2

INGREDIENTS

- 85g wholewheat penne
- 1 tbsp rapeseed oil
- 1 large red pepper , roughly chopped
- 2 frozen, skinless wild salmon fillets (about 120g each)
- 1 lemon , zested and juiced
- 2 garlic cloves , finely grated
- 1 shallot , very finely chopped
- 2 tbsp capers
- 6 pitted Kalamata olives , sliced
- 1 tsp extra virgin olive oil
- 2 handfuls rocket

DIRECTIONS

STEP 1

Cook the pasta following pack instructions. Meanwhile, heat the rapeseed oil in a frying pan, add the pepper, cover and leave for about 5 mins until it softens and starts to char a little. Stir, then push the pepper to one side and add the salmon. Cover and fry for 8-10 mins until just cooked.

STEP 2

Meanwhile, mix the lemon zest and juice in a large bowl with the garlic, shallot, capers and olives.

STEP 3

Add the cooked pepper and salmon to the bowl. Drain the pasta and add it too, with black pepper and the olive oil. Toss everything together, flaking the salmon as you do so. If eating now, toss through the rocket; if packing a lunch, leave to cool, then put in a container with the rocket on top and mix through just before eating.

SLOW COOKER TURKISH BREAKFAST EGGS

Prep: 15 mins - Cook: 5 hrs - 6 hrs - Serves 4

INGREDIENTS

- 1 tbsp olive oil
- 2 onions , finely sliced
- 1 red pepper , cored and finely sliced
- 1 small red chilli , finely sliced
- 8 cherry tomatoes
- 1 slice sourdough bread , cubed
- 4 eggs
- 2 tbsp skimmed milk
- small bunch parsley , finely chopped
- 4 tbsp natural yogurt , to serve

DIRECTIONS

STEP 1

Oil the inside of a small slow cooker and heat if necessary. Heat the remaining oil in a heavy-based frying pan. Stir in the onions, pepper and chilli. Cook until they begin to soften. Tip into the slow cooker and add the cherry tomatoes and bread and stir everything. Season.

STEP 2

Whisk the eggs with the milk and parsley and pour this over the top, making sure all the other ingredients are covered. Cook for 5-6 hours. Serve with the yogurt.

HERB & GARLIC PORK WITH SUMMER RATATOUILLE

Prep: 15 mins - Cook: 25 mins - 4 (or 2 with leftovers for other meals)

INGREDIENTS

- 2 tsp rapeseed oil

- 2 red onions , halved and sliced

- 2 peppers (any colour), diced

- 1 large aubergine , diced

- 2 large courgettes , halved and sliced

- 2 garlic cloves , chopped

- 400g can chopped tomatoes

- 2 tsp vegetable bouillon

- 1 thyme spig

- handful basil , stalks chopped, leaves torn and kept separate

For the pork

- 475g pork tenderloin, fat trimmed off, cut into 2 equal pieces

- 2 garlic cloves , crushed

- 1 tbsp thyme leaves , plus a few sprigs to decorate

- 1 tsp rapeseed oil

- brown rice or new potatoes, to serve

DIRECTIONS

STEP 1

Heat the oil in a large non-stick pan and fry the onions for 5 mins or until softened. Stir in the peppers, aubergine, courgettes and garlic, and cook, stirring, for a few mins. Tip in the tomatoes and 1 can of water, then stir in the bouillon, thyme and basil stalks. Cover and simmer for 20 mins or until tender. Stir through the basil leaves.

STEP 2

Meanwhile, rub the pork with the garlic, then scatter with the thyme and some black pepper, patting it so it sticks all over. Heat the oil in a non-stick frying pan and cook the pork for about 12 mins, turning frequently so it browns on all sides, until tender but still moist. Cover and rest for 5 mins.

STEP 3

If you're making this as part of the Healthy Diet Plan, set aside half of the pork to use in the curried pork bulghar salad later in the week and store in the fridge once cooled. Chill the half of the ratatouille and use it to make the ratatouille pasta salad with rocket for another day. If you are serving four you can skip this step.

STEP 4

To serve, slice the pork and serve with the ratatouille, some brown rice or new potatoes and some extra thyme.

SMASHED CHICKEN WITH CORN SLAW

Prep: 10 mins - Cook: 5 mins - Serves 4

INGREDIENTS

For the chicken

- 4 skinless chicken breast fillets
- 1 lime , zested and juiced
- 2 tbsp bio yogurt
- 1 tsp fresh thyme leaves
- ¼ tsp turmeric
- 2 tbsp finely chopped coriander
- 1 garlic clove , finely grated
- 1 tsp rapeseed oil

For the slaw

- 1 small avocado
- 1 lime , zested and juiced
- 2 tbsp bio yogurt
- 2 tbsp finely chopped coriander
- 160g corn , cut from 2 cobs
- 1 red pepper , deseeded and chopped
- 1 red onion , halved and finely sliced
- 320g white cabbage , finely sliced
- 150g new potatoes , boiled, to serve

DIRECTIONS

STEP 1

Cut the chicken breasts in half, then put them between two sheets of baking parchment and bash with a rolling pin to flatten. Mix the lime zest and juice with the yogurt, thyme, turmeric, coriander and garlic in a large bowl. Add the chicken and stir until well coated. Leave to marinate while you make the slaw.

STEP 2

Mash the avocado with the lime juice and zest, 2 tbsp yogurt and the coriander. Stir in the corn, red pepper, onion and cabbage.

STEP 3

Heat a large non-stick frying pan or griddle pan, then cook the chicken in batches for a few mins each side – they'll cook quickly as they're thin. Serve the hot chicken with the slaw and the new potatoes. If you're cooking for two, chill half the chicken and slaw for lunch another day (eat within two days).

SOUP MAKER TOMATO SOUP

Prep: 5 mins - Cook: 30 mins - Serves 2

INGREDIENTS

- 500g ripe tomatoes , off the vine and quartered or halved
- 1 small onion , chopped
- ½ small carrot , chopped
- ½ celery stick, chopped
- 1 tsp tomato purée
- pinch of sugar
- 450ml vegetable stock

DIRECTIONS

STEP 1

Put all the ingredients into the soup maker and press the 'smooth soup' function. Make sure you don't fill the soup maker above the max fill line.

STEP 2

Once the cycle is complete, season well, and check the soup for sweetness. Add a little more sugar, salt or tomato puree for depth of colour, if you like.

LEEK, TOMATO & BARLEY RISOTTO WITH PAN-COOKED COD

Prep: 10 mins - Cook: 20 mins - Serves 2

INGREDIENTS

- 2 tsp rapeseed oil
- 1 large leek (315g), thinly sliced
- 2 garlic cloves , chopped
- 400g can barley (don't drain)
- 2 tsp vegetable bouillon
- 1 tsp finely chopped sage
- 1 tbsp thyme leaves , plus a few extra to serve

- 160g cherry tomatoes
- 50g finely grated parmesan
- 2 skin-on cod fillets or firm white fish fillets

DIRECTIONS

STEP 1

Heat 1 tsp oil in a non-stick pan and fry the leek and garlic for 5-10 mins, stirring frequently until softened, adding a splash of water to help it cook if you need to.

STEP 2

Tip in the barley with its liquid, then stir in the bouillon, sage and thyme. Simmer, stirring frequently for 3-4 mins. Add the tomatoes and cook about 4-5 mins more until they soften and start to split, adding a drop more water if necessary. Stir in the parmesan.

STEP 3

Meanwhile, heat the remaining oil in a non-stick pan and fry the cod, skin-side down, for 4-5 mins. Flip the fillets over to cook briefly on the other side. Spoon the risotto into two bowls. Serve the cod on top with a few thyme leaves, if you like.

GREEN MINESTRONE WITH TORTELLINI

Prep: 5 mins - Cook: 25 mins - Serves 4

INGREDIENTS

- 2 tbsp olive or rapeseed oil
- 1 onion , chopped
- 1 small leek , chopped
- 1 celery stick , chopped
- 3 garlic cloves , crushed
- 2 bay leaves
- 1l good-quality chicken or vegetable stock
- 100g shredded spring veg or cabbage
- 50g frozen peas
- 1 lemon , zested
- 250g tortellini

DIRECTIONS

STEP 1

Heat the olive or rapeseed oil in a large pan. Add the onion, leek and celery stick. Cook for 8-10 mins until softened, then stir in the garlic and bay leaves. Pour in the chicken or vegetable stock, then cover and simmer for 10 mins. Add the spring veg or cabbage, peas, lemon zest and tortellini (spinach tortellini works well). Cover and cook for another 3 mins, season well and ladle into bowls.

EASY VEGAN PHO

Prep: 10 mins - Cook: 20 mins - Serves 2

INGREDIENTS

- 100g rice noodles
- 1 tsp Marmite
- 1 tsp vegetable oil
- 50g chestnut mushrooms , sliced
- 1 leek , sliced
- 2 tbsp soy sauce

To serve

- 1 red chilli , sliced (deseeded if you don't like it too hot)
- ½ bunch mint , leaves picked and stalk discarded
- handful salted peanuts
- sriracha , to serve

DIRECTIONS

STEP 1

Tip the noodles into a bowl and cover with boiling water. Leave to stand for 10 mins, then drain, rinse in cold water and set aside.

STEP 2

In a jug, mix the Marmite with 500ml boiling water. Set aside while you cook the vegetables.

STEP 3

Heat the oil in a saucepan, then add the mushrooms and leek. Cook for 10-15 mins until softened and beginning to colour, then add the soy sauce and Marmite and water mixture and stir. Bring to the boil for 5 mins.

STEP 4

Divide the noodles between two deep bowls, then ladle over the hot broth. Top with the chilli slices, mint leaves and peanuts, and serve with some sriracha on the side.

ALL-IN–ONE CHICKEN WITH WILTED SPINACH

INGREDIENTS

- 2 beetroot , peeled and cut into small chunks
- 300g celeriac , cut into small chunks
- 2 red onions , quartered
- 8 garlic cloves , 4 crushed, the rest left whole, but peeled
- 1 tbsp rapeseed oil
- 1½ tbsp fresh thyme leaves , plus extra to serve
- 1 lemon , zested and juiced
- 1 tsp fennel seeds
- 1 tsp English mustard powder
- 1 tsp smoked paprika
- 4 tbsp bio yogurt
- 4 bone-in chicken thighs , skin removed
- 260g bag spinach

DIRECTIONS

STEP 1

Heat oven to 200C/180C fan/gas 6. Tip the beetroot, celeriac, onions and whole garlic cloves into a shallow roasting tin. Add the oil, 1 tbsp thyme, half the lemon zest, fennel seeds and a squeeze of lemon juice, then toss together. Roast for 20 mins while you prepare the chicken.

STEP 2

Stir the mustard powder and paprika into 2 tbsp yogurt in a bowl. Add half the crushed garlic, the remaining lemon zest and thyme, and juice from half the lemon. Add the chicken and toss well until it's coated all over. Put the chicken in the tin with the veg and roast for 40 mins until the chicken is cooked through and the vegetables are tender.

STEP 3

About 5 mins before the chicken is ready, wash and drain the spinach and put it in a pan with the remaining crushed garlic. Cook until wilted, then turn off the heat and stir in the remaining yogurt. Scatter some extra thyme over the chicken and vegetables, then serve.

BAKED PIRI-PIRI TILAPIA WITH CRUSHED POTATOES

Prep: 10 mins - Cook: 25 mins - Serves 4

INGREDIENTS

- 600g small new potatoes
- 2 red peppers, cut into chunky pieces
- 1 tbsp red wine vinegar
- drizzle of extra virgin olive oil
- 4 large pieces tilapia or cod
- green salad, to serve

For the piri-piri sauce

- 6 hot pickled peppers (I used Peppadew)
- 1 tsp chilli flakes
- 2 garlic cloves
- juice and zest 1 lemon
- 1 tbsp red wine vinegar
- 2 tbsp extra virgin olive oil
- 1 tbsp smoked paprika

DIRECTIONS

STEP 1

Heat oven to 220C/200C fan/gas 7. Boil the potatoes until knife-tender, then drain. Spread out on a large baking tray and gently crush with the back of a spatula. Add the peppers, drizzle with the vinegar and oil, season well and roast for 25 mins.

STEP 2

Put the piri-piri ingredients in a food processor with some salt. Purée until fine, then pour into a bowl. Put the fish on a baking tray and spoon over some of the piri-piri sauce. Season and bake for the final 10 mins of the potatoes' cooking time. Serve everything with the extra sauce and a green salad on the side.

SEARED BEEF SALAD WITH CAPERS & MINT

Prep: 10 mins - Cook: 12 mins - Serves 2

INGREDIENTS

- 150g new potatoes , thickly sliced
- 160g fine green beans , trimmed and halved
- 160g frozen peas

- rapeseed oil , for brushing
- 200g lean fillet steak , trimmed of any fat
- 160g romaine lettuce , roughly torn into pieces

For the dressing

- 1 tbsp extra virgin olive oil
- 2 tsp cider vinegar
- ½ tsp English mustard powder
- 2 tbsp chopped mint
- 3 tbsp chopped basil
- 1 garlic clove , finely grated
- 1 tbsp capers

DIRECTIONS

STEP 1

Cook the potatoes in a pan of simmering water for 5 mins. Add the beans and cook 5 mins more, then tip in the peas and cook for 2 mins until all the vegetables are just tender. Drain.

STEP 2

Meanwhile, measure all the dressing ingredients in a large bowl and season with black pepper. Stir and crush the herbs and capers with the back of a spoon to intensify their flavours.

STEP 3

Brush a little oil over the steak and grind over some black pepper. Heat a non-stick frying pan over a high heat and cook the steak for 4 mins on one side and 2-3 mins on the other, depending on the thickness and how rare you like it. Transfer to a plate to rest while you carry on with the rest of the salad.

STEP 4

Mix the warm vegetables into the dressing until well coated, then add the lettuce and toss again. Pile onto plates. Slice the steak and turn in any dressing left in the bowl, add to the salad and serve while still warm.

COURGETTE, LEEK & GOAT'S CHEESE SOUP

Prep: 8 mins - Cook: 17 mins - Serves 4

INGREDIENTS

- 1 tbsp rapeseed oil
- 400g leeks, well washed and sliced
- 450g courgettes, sliced

- 3 tsp vegetable bouillon powder, made up to 1 litre with boiling water
- 400g spinach
- 150g tub soft vegetarian goat's cheese
- 15g basil, plus a few leaves to serve
- 8 tsp omega seed mix (see tip)
- 4 x 25g portions wholegrain rye bread

DIRECTIONS

STEP 1

Heat the oil in a large pan and fry the leeks for a few mins to soften. Add the courgettes, then cover the pan and cook for 5 mins more. Pour in the stock, cover and cook for about 7 mins.

STEP 2

Add the spinach, then cover the pan and cook for 5 mins so that it wilts. Take off the heat and blitz until really smooth with a hand blender. Add the goat's cheese and basil, then blitz again.

STEP 3

If you're making this recipe as part of our two-person Summer Healthy Diet Plan, spoon half the soup into two bowls or large flasks, then cool and chill the remainder for another day. Reheat in a pan or microwave to serve. If serving in bowls, scatter with some extra basil leaves and the seeds, and eat with the rye bread.

.

PEA & FETA PEARL BARLEY STEW

Prep: 10 mins - Cook: 45 mins - Serves 4

INGREDIENTS

- 2 tbsp olive oil
- 2 medium onions , chopped
- 2 garlic cloves , chopped
- zest and juice 2 lemons
- 200g pearl barley , rinsed under cold water
- 700ml vegetable stock
- 200g feta , cut into cubes
- ½ small pack mint , leaves shredded, plus a few whole leaves to serve
- 400g frozen peas , defrosted at room temperature

DIRECTIONS

STEP 1

Heat 1 tbsp oil in a pan or flameproof casserole dish over a medium heat. Add the onion and cook for 3 mins, then add the garlic and lemon zest and fry for another 1 min. Add the pearl barley and the stock. Season, bring to the boil, then simmer for 30 mins, stirring occasionally.

STEP 2

Meanwhile, put the feta in a bowl with the remaining olive oil, half the lemon juice, most of the mint and a good grinding of black pepper. Leave to marinate while the barley cooks.

STEP 3

Remove the lid from the barley and cook for 5 mins more. Increase the heat then add the peas, half the feta and all the feta juices. Cook for 3 mins, then check the seasoning. Divide between four bowls and top with the remaining feta and mint.

MARINATED LAMB STEAKS WITH BARLEY SALAD

Prep: 15 mins - Cook: 30 mins Plus marinating - Serves 2

INGREDIENTS

- 2 tbsp olive oil
- 2 garlic cloves , finely chopped
- pinch dried chilli flakes
- small bunch mint , chopped
- 2 lean lamb leg steaks, about 100g/4oz each, trimmed of any fat
- 100g pearl barley
- 200g broad beans , fresh or frozen, podded and skins removed, if you like
- 100g frozen petits pois
- 1 small red onion , finely chopped
- zest and juice 1 lemon

DIRECTIONS

STEP 1

Mix together 1 tbsp oil, the garlic, chilli, half the mint and some salt and pepper. Rub all over the steaks, then if you have time, leave to marinate for up to 2 hrs.

STEP 2

Cook the pearl barley in boiling, salted water until tender, but not too soft, about 20 mins. Cook the beans and peas in the same pan for the last 2 mins. Drain really well, then tip into a large bowl. Add the red onion, remaining mint, lemon zest and juice, remaining oil, salt and pepper. Toss everything together.

STEP 3

Heat a griddle or frying pan until almost smoking and cook the lamb for 4 mins on each side for pink, or longer if you prefer your meat well done. Divide the barley salad between 2 plates and serve with the grilled lamb, drizzled with any pan juices.

COURGETTE LASAGNE

Prep: 20 mins - Cook: 1 hr and 25 mins - Serves 6

INGREDIENTS

- 8 plum tomatoes , halved
- 2 garlic cloves , lightly bashed
- 1 tbsp olive oil
- 1 rosemary sprig
- ½ tbsp golden caster sugar
- 2 leeks , sliced into rings
- 20g unsalted butter
- 100g baby spinach
- 500g courgettes , grated
- 10 lasagne sheets
- 250g tub of ricotta
- 125g mozzarella , torn
- 50g parmesan (or vegetarian alternative), grated

DIRECTIONS

STEP 1

Heat oven to 200C/180C fan/gas 6. Put the tomatoes on a baking tray with the garlic, oil, rosemary and a good pinch of seasoning. Bake for 25-30 mins until soft, then discard the rosemary and peel off the garlic skin. Put the tomatoes, garlic and sugar in a blender and blitz a few times until you have a chunky sauce.

STEP 2

Meanwhile, put the leeks in a pan over a low heat, add the butter, season and cook for 7-10 mins or until soft. Add the spinach and courgettes, and cook, covered, for 2 mins until wilted and soft. Set aside.

STEP 3

In a lasagne dish, layer up the ingredients using the tomato sauce first, then some pasta, followed by the ricotta and vegetables. Keep layering until you've used up everything. Finish with a final layer of the vegetables, the mozzarella and the Parmesan. Bake in the oven for 40-45 mins until the sauce has reduced and the top is golden brown.

VEGGIE OLIVE WRAPS WITH MUSTARD VINAIGRETTE

Prep: 10 mins no cook - Serves 1

INGREDIENTS

- 1 carrot , shredded or coarsely grated
- 80g wedge red cabbage , finely shredded
- 2 spring onions , thinly sliced
- 1 courgette , shredded or coarsely grated
- handful basil leaves
- 5 green olives , pitted and halved
- ½ tsp English mustard powder
- 2 tsp extra virgin rapeseed oil
- 1 tbsp cider vinegar
- 1 large seeded tortilla

DIRECTIONS

STEP 1

Mix all the ingredients except for the tortilla and toss well.

STEP 2

Put the tortilla on a sheet of foil and pile the filling along one side of the wrap – it will almost look like too much mixture, but once you start to roll it firmly it will compact. Roll the tortilla from the filling side, folding in the sides as you go. Fold the foil in at the ends to keep stuff inside the wrap. Cut in half and eat straight away. If taking to work, leave whole and wrap up like a cracker in baking parchment.

RUSTIC VEGETABLE SOUP

Prep: 15 mins - Cook: 30 mins - Serves 4

INGREDIENTS

- 1 tbsp rapeseed oil
- 1 large onion, chopped
- 2 carrots, chopped
- 2 celery sticks, chopped
- 50g dried red lentils

- 1½ l boiling vegetable bouillon (we used Marigold)
- 2 tbsp tomato purée
- 1 tbsp chopped fresh thyme
- 1 leek, finely sliced
- 175g bite-sized cauliflower florets
- 1 courgette, chopped
- 3 garlic cloves, finely chopped
- ½ large Savoy cabbage, stalks removed and leaves chopped
- 1 tbsp basil, chopped

DIRECTIONS

STEP 1

Heat the oil in a large pan with a lid. Add the onion, carrots and celery and fry for 10 mins, stirring from time to time until they are starting to colour a little around the edges. Stir in the lentils and cook for 1 min more.

STEP 2

Pour in the hot bouillon, add the tomato purée and thyme and stir well. Add the leek, cauliflower, courgette, and garlic, bring to the boil, then cover and leave to simmer for 15 mins.

STEP 3

Add the cabbage and basil and cook for 5 mins more until the veg is just tender. Season with pepper, ladle into bowls and serve. Will keep in the fridge for a couple of days. Freezes well. Thaw, then reheat in a pan until piping hot.

CUCUMBER, PEA & LETTUCE SOUP

Prep: 5 - mins Cook: 15 mins - Serves 4

INGREDIENTS

- 1 tsp rapeseed oil
- small bunch spring onions , roughly chopped
- 1 cucumber , roughly chopped
- 1 large round lettuce , roughly chopped
- 225g frozen peas
- 4 tsp vegetable bouillon
- 4 tbsp bio yogurt (optional)
- 4 slices rye bread

DIRECTIONS

STEP 1

Boil 1.4 litres water in a kettle. Heat the oil in a large non-stick frying pan and cook the spring onions for 5 mins, stirring frequently, or until softened. Add the cucumber, lettuce and peas, then pour in the boiled water. Stir in the bouillon, cover and simmer for 10 mins or until the vegetables are soft but still bright green.

STEP 2

Blitz the mixture with a hand blender until smooth. Serve hot or cold, topped with yogurt (if you like), with rye bread alongside.

PENNE WITH BROCCOLI, LEMON & ANCHOVIES

Prep: 10 mins - Cook: 17 mins - Serves 2

INGREDIENTS

- 170g wholemeal penne
- 1 leek , washed and sliced
- 180g broccoli , cut into small florets
- 2 tsp oil from the anchovy can, plus 15g anchovies, chopped
- 1 red pepper , seeded, quartered and sliced
- ½ tsp finely chopped rosemary
- 1 red chilli , seeded and sliced
- 3 garlic cloves , sliced
- ½ lemon , zested and juiced
- 4 tbsp ricotta
- 2 tbsp sunflower seeds

DIRECTIONS

STEP 1

Boil the pasta with the sliced leek for 7 mins, then add the broccoli and boil for 5 mins until everything is just tender.

STEP 2

Meanwhile, heat the oil from the anchovies and fry the red pepper with the rosemary, chilli and garlic in a large non-stick pan for 5 mins until softened.

STEP 3

Drain the pasta, reserving a little water, then tip the pasta and veg into the pan and add the lemon juice and zest, anchovies and ricotta. Toss well over the heat, using the pasta water to moisten. Toss through the sunflower seeds and serve.

RED LENTIL, CHICKPEA & CHILLI SOUP

Prep: 10 mins - Cook: 25 mins - Serves 4

INGREDIENTS

- 2 tsp cumin seeds
- large pinch chilli flakes
- 1 tbsp olive oil
- 1 red onion, chopped
- 140g red split lentils
- 850ml vegetable stock or water
- 400g can tomatoes, whole or chopped
- 200g can chickpeas or ½ a can, drained and rinsed (freeze leftovers)
- small bunch coriander, roughly chopped (save a few leaves, to serve)
- 4 tbsp 0% Greek yogurt, to serve

DIRECTIONS

STEP 1

Heat a large saucepan and dry-fry 2 tsp cumin seeds and a large pinch of chilli flakes for 1 min, or until they start to jump around the pan and release their aromas.

STEP 2

Add 1 tbsp olive oil and 1 chopped red onion, and cook for 5 mins.

STEP 3

Stir in 140g red split lentils, 850ml vegetable stock or water and a 400g can tomatoes, then bring to the boil. Simmer for 15 mins until the lentils have softened.

STEP 4

Whizz the soup with a stick blender or in a food processor until it is a rough purée, pour back into the pan and add a 200g can drained and rinsed chickpeas.

STEP 5

Heat gently, season well and stir in a small bunch of chopped coriander, reserving a few leaves to serve. Finish with 4 tbsp 0% Greek yogurt and extra coriander leaves.

CHINESE CHICKEN NOODLE SOUP WITH PEANUT SAUCE

Prep: 15 mins - Cook: 30 mins - Serves 2

INGREDIENTS

- 1 tbsp sunflower oil
- 4 skinless boneless chicken thighs
- 1 garlic clove , crushed
- 1 thumb-sized piece ginger , grated
- 500ml chicken stock
- 1 tsp soy sauce
- ½ hispi cabbage , finely sliced
- 150g mushrooms
- 150g straight to wok noodles (we used udon)

For the peanut sauce

- 1 tbsp peanut butter
- 1 tsp soy sauce
- 1 tsp honey
- sriracha or other chilli sauce (optional), to serve

DIRECTIONS

STEP 1

Heat the oil in a saucepan over a medium heat, add the chicken and brown a little, so around 2-3 mins, then add the garlic and ginger and stir to coat the chicken. Fry for a further minute, then pour in the chicken stock and soy, bring to the boil, then reduce to a simmer. Cover with a lid and leave to gently bubble for 25-30 mins until the chicken is tender and pulls apart.

STEP 2

Meanwhile, mix the sauce ingredients with a splash of water. When the chicken is ready, lift it out with a slotted spoon and use two forks to shred it on a plate. Add the cabbage, mushrooms and noodles to the pan, turn up the heat, then stir in the chicken, add a dash of sriracha, if using, and ladle into bowls. Top with a drizzle of the peanut sauce and serve.

CHICKEN & BROCCOLI POTATO-TOPPED PIE

Prep: 35 mins - Cook: 1 hr and 25 mins - Serves 4

INGREDIENTS

- 750g potatoes, peeled and halved
- 250g broccoli, cut into small florets
- 100ml strong chicken stock
- small bunch tarragon, finely chopped (optional)
- 1-2 tsp Dijon mustard
- 100g frozen peas
- 1 tbsp butter

For the chicken base

- 25g butter
- 25g plain flour
- 250ml milk
- 1 tsp olive oil
- 2-3 (depending on size) skinless chicken thigh fillets, cut into cubes
- 1 skinless chicken breast, cut into cubes
- ⅓ onion, very finely chopped (optional)

DIRECTIONS

STEP 1

For the base, melt the butter in a saucepan, stir in the flour and cook for a few mins, stirring all the time. Now, using a whisk or spatula, carefully stir in the milk, a little at a time, making sure the sauce stays smooth. Bring the mixture to a simmer and cook for a couple of mins until it thickens – it will be very thick. Turn the heat right down and keep cooking for 5 mins, stirring often.

STEP 2

Meanwhile, heat the oil in a non-stick frying pan and fry all of the chicken in batches until it starts to colour lightly at the edges. Scoop out each batch of chicken and put it on a plate. Add the onion to the pan if you are using it, and cook over a low heat until soft. Add the chicken and any juices and the onion to the white sauce, fold it in and cook the mixture for a further 15 mins or until the chicken is cooked through. If you're making the base ahead of time, you can leave it to cool at this stage then freeze in an airtight container for up to a month. (Defrost fully before using in the next step.)

STEP 3

Heat oven to 180C/160C fan/gas 4. Cook the potatoes in boiling water for 10 mins, then drain and cool a little before slicing thickly.

STEP 4

Meanwhile, cook the broccoli until tender, then drain. Heat the chicken base with the stock in a pan until it is just beginning to bubble, then stir in the tarragon (if using) and the mustard. Fold in the broccoli and peas. Tip the chicken mixture into a dish and arrange the potato slices on top, then dot the butter over. Bake for 30-35 mins or until golden.

CRAB & LEMON SPAGHETTI WITH PEAS

Prep: 7 mins - Cook: 12 mins - Serves 2

INGREDIENTS

- 150g wholemeal spaghetti
- 1 tbsp rapeseed oil
- 2 leeks (220g), cut into lengths then long thin strips
- 1 red chilli , deseeded and finely chopped
- 1 garlic clove , finely grated
- 160g frozen peas
- 1 lemon , zested and 1/2 juiced
- 100g fresh white and brown crabmeat (not dressed)

DIRECTIONS

STEP 1

Cook the spaghetti for 12 mins, or following pack instructions, until al dente. Meanwhile, heat the oil in a large frying pan, add the leeks and chilli and cook for 5 mins. Stir in the garlic, peas, lemon zest and juice, then cook for a few mins.

STEP 2

Drain the pasta, then add to the pan with ¼ mug of pasta water and the crab, then toss everything together until well coated. Spoon into shallow bowls and serve.

GARLICKY MUSHROOM PENNE

Prep: 20 mins - Cook: 15 mins - Serves 2

INGREDIENTS

- 210g can chickpeas , no need to drain
- 1 tbsp lemon juice

- 1 large garlic clove

- 1 tsp vegetable bouillon

- 2 tsp tahini

- ¼ tsp ground coriander

- 115g wholemeal penne

- 2 tsp rapeseed oil

- 2 red onions , halved and sliced

- 200g closed cup mushrooms , roughly chopped

- ½ lemon , juiced

- generous handful chopped parsley

DIRECTIONS

STEP 1

To make the hummus, tip a 210g can chickpeas with the liquid into a bowl and add 1 tbsp lemon juice, 1 large garlic clove, 1 tsp vegetable bouillon, 2 tsp tahini and ¼ tsp ground coriander.

STEP 2

Blitz to a wet paste with a hand blender, still retaining some texture from the chickpeas.

STEP 3

Cook 115g wholemeal penne pasta according to the pack instructions.

STEP 4

Meanwhile, heat 2 tsp rapeseed oil in a non-stick wok or large frying pan and add 2 halved and sliced red onions and 200g roughly chopped closed cup mushrooms, stirring frequently until softened and starting to caramelise.

STEP 5

Toss together lightly, squeeze over the juice of ½ a lemon and serve, adding a dash of water to loosen the mixture a little if needed. Scatter with a generous handful of chopped parsley.

AVOCADO & BEAN TRIANGLES

Prep: 5 mins - No cook - Serves 2

INGREDIENTS

- 3 triangluar bread thins

- 210g can red kidney beans , drained

- 1 tbsp finely chopped dill , plus extra for garnish

- 1/2 lemon , for squeezing

- 1 tomato , chopped

- 1 small avocado
- 1 small red onion , finely chopped

DIRECTIONS

STEP 1

Follow our triangular bread thins recipe to make your own. While they bake, roughly mash the beans with the dill and a good squeeze of lemon then stir in the tomato.

STEP 2

Cut the bread triangles in half and top with the beans. Scoop the avocado into a bowl and roughly mash with a squeeze more lemon. Spoon the avocado onto the beans, scatter over the chopped onion, then garnish with the remaining dill.

BUCKWHEAT WITH CHARRED BABY AUBERGINES

Prep: 15 - mins Cook: 20 mins - Serves 4

INGREDIENTS

- 350g baby aubergines , halved
- 8 whole spring onions , tops trimmed
- 250g buckwheat
- 2 tbsp cold pressed rapeseed oil
- 1 x 400g can green lentils , drained
- 30g dried cherries , roughly chopped
- 8 walnut halves, finely chopped
- 1 lemon , juiced
- ½ tsp chilli flakes
- small bunch dill , finely chopped
- 30g soft goat's cheese , crumbled

DIRECTIONS

STEP 1

Heat the grill to its highest setting. Spread the aubergines out on a baking sheet, cut-side up, and grill for 10-15 mins until they begin to soften and blister.

STEP 2

Meanwhile, heat a griddle pan over a high heat. Add the spring onions and cook on each side for 5-6 mins until softened and charred. Remove with tongs and set aside.

STEP 3

Bring a medium-sized pan of water to the boil. Tip the buckwheat into a frying pan and dry fry over a medium heat for 3 mins until lightly toasted. Add the buckwheat to the boiling water and cook for 4-5 mins. Drain and toss with the oil. Leave to cool down for 5 mins.

STEP 4

Toss the warm buckwheat, lentils, cherries, walnuts, lemon juice, chilli and most of the dill in a bowl. Spread out on a serving plate and top with the aubergines, charred spring onions, remaining dill and goat's cheese.

STEAMED SALMON & VEG RICE BOWL

Prep: 10 mins - Cook: 15 mins - 20 mins - Serves 4

INGREDIENTS

- 200g brown rice
- 100g green beans
- 200g pak choi , chopped into chunky pieces
- 4 x 100g salmon fillets
- For the dressing
- 4 tbsp kecap manis (sweet soy sauce)
- juice 3 limes
- 2 tbsp sambal oelek (chopped chilli in a jar) or 1 red chilli, deseeded and chopped
- 1 tbsp rice vinegar
- 1 tbsp golden caster sugar
- To serve
- 4 spring onions , finely chopped
- 4 tbsp mixed seeds (I used pumpkin, sesame and sunflower)
- pickled ginger , chopped (optional)

DIRECTIONS

STEP 1

In a small bowl, mix together the dressing ingredients, then set aside. Boil the rice in plenty of water and drain when just cooked, about 15 mins.

STEP 2

Meanwhile, put the vegetables and fish in a large steamer in two layers. Steam the fish for 5-8 mins and the veg for 4-5 mins until cooked through. Spoon the rice into bowls and top with the steamed fish and veg. Pour some dressing over and top with the spring onions, mixed seeds and pickled ginger, if you like.

CARAMELISED ONION & GOAT'S CHEESE PIZZA

Prep: 20 mins - Cook: 30 mins - Serves 2

INGREDIENTS

For the base

- 125g wholemeal flour , plus a little for kneading if necessary
- ½ tsp instant yeast
- pinch of salt
- 1 tsp rapeseed oil , plus extra for greasing

For the topping

- 2 onions , halved and thinly sliced
- 2 tsp rapeseed oil
- 2 tsp balsamic vinegar
- 160g baby spinach leaves (not the very tiny ones), chopped
- 2 large garlic cloves , finely grated
- 50g soft goat's cheese
- 4 pitted Kalamata olives , quartered
- few soft thyme leaves
- 1 tsp sunflower seeds

DIRECTIONS

STEP 1

Heat oven to 220C/200C fan/gas 7. Tip the flour into a mixer with a dough hook, or a bowl. Add the yeast, salt, oil and just under 100ml warm water then mix to a soft dough. Knead in the food mixer for about 5 mins, but if making this by hand, tip onto a work surface and knead for about 10 mins. The dough is sticky, but try not to add too much extra flour. Leave in the bowl and cover with a tea towel while you make the topping. There is no need to let the dough prove for a specific time – just let it sit while you get on with the next step.

STEP 2

Tip the onions into a non-stick wok and add the oil, 4 tbsp water and balsamic vinegar. Cover with a saucepan lid that sits inside the pan to help the onions soften, then cook for 15 mins, stirring about 3 times and replacing the lid quickly so as not to lose too much moisture. After the time is up, the onions should be golden and all the liquid gone. Tip onto a plate. Add the spinach and garlic to the pan and stir-fry until the spinach has wilted.

STEP 3

Take the dough from the bowl and cut in half with an oiled knife, then press each piece into a 25-15 cm oval on a large greased baking sheet with oiled hands. Don't knead the dough first otherwise it will be too elastic and it will keep shrinking back.

STEP 4

Spread with the spinach followed by the onions, then dot with the cheese and scatter with the olives, thyme and sunflower seeds. Bake for 15 mins until golden and the base is cooked through.

CHILLI TEMPEH STIR-FRY

Prep: 10 mins - Cook: 15 mins - Serves 2

INGREDIENTS

- 300g long-stem broccoli
- ½ tbsp toasted sesame oil
- 150g tempeh , sliced and cut into 2cm cubes
- 2 garlic cloves , thinly sliced
- 1 thumb-sized piece ginger , peeled and finely grated
- ½ small red chilli , deseeded and finely chopped
- ½ tbsp gochujang paste
- 1 tsp sesame seeds
- steamed brown rice , to serve (optional)

DIRECTIONS

STEP 1

Boil the broccoli for 1 min 30 secs. Drain.

STEP 2

Heat the oil in a non-stick pan. Stir-fry the tempeh for 2-3 mins, then put on a plate. Fry the garlic, ginger and chilli for 2 mins. Tip in the broccoli and toss.

STEP 3

Mix the gochujang with 2 tbsp water and the tempeh. Add to the pan with the seeds. Cook for 2 mins. Serve with rice, if you like.

BEEF GOULASH SOUP

Prep: 15 mins - Cook: 1 hr - Serves 2 - 3

INGREDIENTS

- 1 tbsp rapeseed oil
- 1 large onion, halved and sliced
- 3 garlic cloves, sliced
- 200g extra lean stewing beef, finely diced
- 1 tsp caraway seeds
- 2 tsp smoked paprika
- 400g can chopped tomatoes
- 600ml beef stock
- 1 medium sweet potato, peeled and diced
- 1 green pepper, deseeded and diced

Supercharged topping

- 150g pot natural bio yogurt
- good handful parsley, chopped

DIRECTIONS

STEP 1

Heat the oil in a large pan, add the onion and garlic, and fry for 5 mins until starting to colour. Stir in the beef, increase the heat and fry, stirring, to brown it.

STEP 2

Add the caraway and paprika, stir well, then tip in the tomatoes and stock. Cover and leave to cook gently for 30 mins.

STEP 3

Stir in the sweet potato and green pepper, cover and cook for 20 mins more or until tender. Allow to cool a little, then serve topped with the yogurt and parsley (if the soup is too hot, it will kill the beneficial bacteria in the yogurt).

SPINACH & CHICKPEA CURRY

Prep: 5 mins - Cook: 15 mins - Serves 4

INGREDIENTS

- 2 tbsp mild curry paste
- 1 onion, chopped
- 400g can cherry tomatoes
- 2 x 400g cans chickpeas, drained and rinsed
- 250g bag baby leaf spinach

- squeeze lemon juice
- basmati rice, to serve

DIRECTIONS

STEP 1

Heat the curry paste in a large non-stick frying pan. Once it starts to split, add the onion and cook for 2 mins to soften. Tip in the tomatoes and bubble for 5 mins or until the sauce has reduced.

STEP 2

Add the chickpeas and some seasoning, then cook for 1 min more. Take off the heat, then tip in the spinach and allow the heat of the pan to wilt the leaves. Season, add the lemon juice, and serve with basmati rice.

CREAMY SPROUT, HAZELNUT & LEEK PASTA

Prep: 15 mins - Cook: 25 mins - Serves 4

INGREDIENTS

- ½ tbsp rapeseed oil
- 3 leeks , halved and sliced
- 200g Brussels sprouts , ½ chopped and ½ quartered
- 2 garlic cloves , rushed
- 50ml low-salt vegetable stock
- 3 tbsp low-fat crème fraîche
- 350g short pasta (riciolli or fusilli work well)
- 1 tbsp grated parmesan or veggie alternative
- 1 lemon , zested
- ½ small bunch of parsley , finely chopped
- 1 tbsp chopped hazelnuts , toasted

DIRECTIONS

STEP 1

Heat the oil in a large frying pan over a low heat. Add the leeks and sprouts and cook for 10-15 mins or until softened. Add the garlic and cook for 1 min. Stir through the hot stock and crème fraîche.

STEP 2

Cook the pasta following pack instructions. Drain and toss with the leeks and sprouts, parmesan, lemon, parsley and hazelnuts, adding a ladleful of the pasta cooking water if needed to loosen. Season to taste and spoon into four bowls.

SLOW COOKER WHOLE CHICKEN

Prep: **15 mins** - Cook: **5 hrs - Serves 6**

INGREDIENTS

- 1 large chicken

DIRECTIONS

STEP 1

Heat the slow cooker if necessary and add a splash of water to the base. Scrunch up some foil to make a trivet to sit in the base of the bowl to rest the chicken on. Put the chicken into the pot and season the skin. Cover and cook on Low for 5 hours or until the leg or wing feels very loose when you wiggle it. Tip the juices inside the chicken out as you lift it out.

STEP 2

Brown the chicken skin under the grill or carve the chicken before anyone sees it. Spoon the liquid out of the base of the pan to use as gravy, there won't be much but it will have a good flavour.

SPICY HARISSA CHICKEN WITH LENTILS

Prep: **10 mins |Cook: 45 mins - Serves 4**

INGREDIENTS

- 1 tbsp olive oil
- 1 red onion , chopped
- 1 garlic clove , crushed
- 50g harissa
- 500g chicken thigh , skin removed, boned and diced
- 1 medium carrot , grated
- 200g dried puy lentils
- 2 x 400g cans chopped tomatoes
- 1.2l stock , made from 1 chicken or vegetable stock cube
- flat-leaf parsley , to serve (optional)

DIRECTIONS

STEP 1

Heat the oil in a large frying pan. Fry the onion on a low heat for 5-6 mins until softened and translucent. Add the garlic and cook for 1 min more.

STEP 2

Stir in the harissa, add the chicken and cook until well browned all over. Stir in the carrot, lentils and tomatoes, then add the stock so the chicken is fully immersed.

STEP 3

Reduce the heat and cook, uncovered, for 30-35 mins until the chicken is thoroughly cooked, and the lentils are tender and have absorbed the liquid. Season well, scatter with parsley (if using) and serve.

MEXICAN CHICKEN STEW

Prep: 20 mins - Cook: 25 mins - Serves 4

INGREDIENTS

- 1 tbsp vegetable oil
- 1 medium onion, finely chopped
- 3 garlic cloves, finely chopped
- ½ tsp dark brown sugar
- 1 tsp chipotle paste (we used Discovery)
- 400g can chopped tomatoes
- 4 skinless, boneless chicken breasts
- 1 small red onion, sliced into rings
- a few coriander leaves
- corn tortillas, or rice to serve

DIRECTIONS

STEP 1

Heat the oil in a medium saucepan. Add the onion and cook for 5 mins or until softened and starting to turn golden, adding the garlic for the final min. Stir in the sugar, chipotle paste and tomatoes. Put the chicken into the pan, spoon over the sauce, and simmer gently for 20 mins until the chicken has cooked (add a splash of water if the sauce gets too dry).

STEP 2

Remove the chicken from the pan and shred with 2 forks, then stir back into the sauce. Scatter with a little red onion, the coriander, and serve with remaining red onion, tortillas or rice.

STEP 3

If you want to use a slow cooker, cook the onion and garlic as above, then put into your slow cooker with the sugar, chipotle, tomatoes and chicken. Cover and cook on High for 2 hours. Remove the chicken and shred then serve as above.

HARISSA SALMON WITH ZESTY COUSCOUS

Prep: 10 mins - Cook: 15 mins - Serves 2

INGREDIENTS

- 2 skinless salmon fillets
- zest and juice 1 orange
- 1 tbsp olive oil
- 1-2 tsp rose harissa (depending on how spicy you like it)
- 100g couscous
- ¼ cucumber , finely diced
- 1 small red onion , finely diced
- small pack parsley , chopped, or 1/2 handful mint
- 1 tbsp flaked almond , toasted (optional)

DIRECTIONS

STEP 1

Heat oven to 200C/180C fan/gas 6 and arrange the salmon in a shallow ovenproof dish. Mix the orange juice with the oil and harissa, then pour over the salmon and bake for 10-12 mins until the fish flakes easily, but is still moist.

STEP 2

Meanwhile, put the couscous in a pan with the orange zest, 200ml water and a sprinkling of salt. Heat until the water bubbles round the edges of the pan, then cover and turn off the heat. After 5 mins, tip the couscous into a bowl, add the cucumber, onion, parsley and almonds (if using) and toss together ready to serve with the salmon and spicy juices.

BROCCOLI AND KALE GREEN SOUP

Prep: 15 mins - Cook: 20 mins - Serves 2

INGREDIENTS

- 500ml stock , made by mixing 1 tbsp bouillon powder and boiling water in a jug
- 1 tbsp sunflower oil
- 2 garlic cloves , sliced
- thumb-sized piece ginger , sliced
- ½ tsp ground coriander

- 3cm/1in piece fresh turmeric root, peeled and grated, or 1/2 tsp ground turmeric
- pinch of pink Himalayan salt
- 200g courgettes , roughly sliced
- 85g broccoli
- 100g kale , chopped
- 1 lime , zested and juiced
- small pack parsley , roughly chopped, reserving a few whole leaves to serve

DIRECTIONS

STEP 1

Put the oil in a deep pan, add the garlic, ginger, coriander, turmeric and salt, fry on a medium heat for 2 mins, then add 3 tbsp water to give a bit more moisture to the spices.

STEP 2

Add the courgettes, making sure you mix well to coat the slices in all the spices, and continue cooking for 3 mins. Add 400ml stock and leave to simmer for 3 mins.

STEP 3

Add the broccoli, kale and lime juice with the rest of the stock. Leave to cook again for another 3-4 mins until all the vegetables are soft.

STEP 4

Take off the heat and add the chopped parsley. Pour everything into a blender and blend on high speed until smooth. It will be a beautiful green with bits of dark speckled through (which is the kale). Garnish with lime zest and parsley.

HEALTHY BANANA BREAD

Prep: 20 mins - Cook: 1 hr and 15 mins - Cuts into 10 slices

INGREDIENTS

- low-fat spread, for the tin, plus extra to serve
- 140g wholemeal flour
- 100g self-raising flour
- 1 tsp bicarbonate of soda
- 1 tsp baking powder
- 300g mashed banana from overripe black bananas
- 4 tbsp agave syrup
- 3 large eggs, beaten with a fork
- 150ml pot low-fat natural yogurt

- 25g chopped pecan or walnuts (optional)

DIRECTIONS

STEP 1

Heat oven to 160C/140C fan/gas 3. Grease and line a 2lb loaf tin with baking parchment (allow it to come 2cm above top of tin). Mix the flours, bicarb, baking powder and a pinch of salt in a large bowl.

STEP 2

Mix the bananas, syrup, eggs and yogurt. Quickly stir into dry ingredients, then gently scrape into the tin and scatter with nuts, if using. Bake for 1 hr 10 mins-1 hr 15 mins or until a skewer comes out clean.

STEP 3

Cool in tin on a wire rack. Eat warm or at room temperature, with low-fat spread.

EASY CREAMY COLESLAW

Prep: 20 mins - No cook - Serves 4

INGREDIENTS

- ½ white cabbage , shredded
- 2 carrots , grated
- 4 spring onions , chopped
- 2 tbsp sultanas
- 3 tbsp low-fat mayonnaise
- 1 tbsp wholegrain mustard

DIRECTIONS

STEP 1

Put the cabbage, carrots, spring onions and sultanas in a large bowl and stir to combine.

STEP 2

Mix the mayonnaise with the mustard in another small bowl and drizzle over the veg. Fold everything together to coat in the creamy sauce, then season to taste.

TERIYAKI PORK MEATBALLS

Prep: 1 min - Cook: 13 mins - Serves 4

INGREDIENTS

- 250g dried medium egg noodles
- 12 fresh pork meatballs
- 300g pak choi
- 6 tbsp teriyaki sauce

DIRECTIONS

STEP 1

Cook the noodles following pack instructions. Add 2 tbsp sunflower oil to a frying pan over a medium heat. Fry the meatballs for 3 mins or until golden brown all over. Lower the heat and cook for 6 mins more. Quarter the pak choi, raise the heat, add the pak choi and cook for 3 mins. Stir through the teriyaki sauce and toss everything together with the drained noodles. Divide between bowls and serve.

CREAMY SQUASH LINGUINE

Prep: 5 mins - Cook: 1 hr - Serves 4

INGREDIENTS

- 350g chopped butternut squash
- 3 peeled garlic cloves
- 3 tbsp olive oil
- 350g linguine
- small bunch sage

DIRECTIONS

STEP 1

Heat oven to 200C/180C fan/gas 6. Put the squash and garlic on a baking tray and drizzle with the olive oil. Roast for 35-40 mins until soft. Season.

STEP 2

Cook the pasta according to pack instructions. Drain, reserving the water. Use a stick blender to whizz the squash with 400ml cooking water. Heat some oil in a frying pan, fry the sage until crisp, then drain on kitchen paper. Tip the pasta and sauce into the pan and warm through. Scatter with sage.

BARLEY & BROCCOLI RISOTTO WITH LEMON & BASIL

Prep: 10 mins - Cook: 35 mins plus overnight soaking - Serves 2

INGREDIENTS

- 100g wholegrain pearl barley
- 2 tsp reduced-salt vegetable bouillon powder
- 2 tbsp rapeseed oil
- 1 large leek , chopped
- 2 garlic cloves

- ⅔ pack basil
- generous squeeze of lemon juice
- 125g Tenderstem broccoli from a 200g pack

DIRECTIONS

STEP 1

Pour a litre of cold water over the barley, cover and leave to soak overnight.

STEP 2

The next day, drain the barley, reserve the liquid and use it to make 500ml vegetable bouillon. Heat half the oil in a non-stick pan, add the leek and cook briefly to soften. Tip half into a bowl, then add the barley and bouillon to the pan, cover and simmer for 20 mins.

STEP 3

Meanwhile, add the garlic, basil, remaining oil, the lemon juice and 3 tbsp water to the leeks in the bowl, and blitz to a paste with a stick blender

STEP 4

When the barley has cooked for 20 mins, add the broccoli to the pan and cook for 5-10 mins more until both are tender. Stir in the basil purée, heat very briefly (to retain the fragrance), then spoon into bowls to serve.

MELON WITH MINT & FETA

Serves 2

INGREDIENTS

- 2 x 5cm wedges of watermelon
- 40g feta , crumbled
- handful chopped mint
- 2 wedges of lime

DIRECTIONS

STEP 1

Take each wedge of melon and slice between the rind and flesh to separate them, then cut downwards to make bite-size chunks. Flick out the seeds, scatter over the feta and mint, and squeeze over the lime before serving.

VEGETARIAN BOLOGNESE

Prep: 10 mins - Cook: 1 hr - Serves 4

INGREDIENTS

- 2 tbsp olive oil

- 1 medium onion , finely chopped
- 2 carrots , very finely chopped
- 2 celery sticks , very finely chopped
- 1 garlic clove , crushed
- 350g frozen Quorn mince
- 1 bay leaf
- 500ml passata
- 1 good-quality vegetable stock cube
- 100ml milk
- small bunch basil , chopped
- 600g cooked spaghetti or other pasta shape (about 250g dried)
- vegetarian hard cheese , to serve

DIRECTIONS

STEP 1

Heat the oil in a saucepan and gently fry the onion, carrots and celery until the onion is starting to soften. Stir in the garlic and the Quorn (there's no need to defrost it) and fry for a couple of mins. Add the bay leaf, passata, vegetable stock cube and 200ml water, then bring everything to the boil.

STEP 2

Turn down the heat and simmer for 30 mins or until all the pieces of veg are tender and disappearing into the tomato sauce. Add the milk, then cover with a lid and cook for 10 mins. Season to taste. If the sauce is a bit thin, keep bubbling until it thickens. Stir through the basil. Serve with the spaghetti and grate the cheese over the top, if you like. Can be frozen into portions and reheated.

PIZZA SAUCE

Prep: 5 mins - Cook: 50 mins - makes 4-6 pizzas

INGREDIENTS

- 2 tbsp olive oil
- 1 small onion, finely chopped
- 1 fat garlic clove, crushed
- 2 x 400g cans chopped tomatoes
- 3 tbsp tomato purée
- 1 bay leaf
- 2 tbsp dried oregano
- 2 tsp brown sugar

- 1 small bunch basil, finely chopped

DIRECTIONS

STEP 1

Heat the oil in a saucepan over a low heat, then add the onion along with a generous pinch of salt. Fry gently for 12-15 mins or until the onion has softened and is turning translucent. Add the garlic and fry for a further min. Tip in the tomatoes and purée along with the bay, oregano and sugar. Bring to the boil and lower the heat. Simmer, uncovered, for 30-35 mins or until thickened and reduced. Season. For a really smooth sauce, blitz with a stick blender, otherwise leave as is.

STEP 2

Stir the basil into the sauce. The sauce will cover 4-6 large pizza bases. Keeps well in the fridge for 1 week or stored in a container in the freezer.

CURRIED COD

Prep: 10 mins - Cook: 25 mins - Serves 4

INGREDIENTS

- 1 tbsp oil
- 1 onion, chopped
- 2 tbsp medium curry powder
- thumb-sized piece ginger, peeled and finely grated
- 3 garlic cloves, crushed
- 2 x 400g cans chopped tomatoes
- 400g can chickpeas
- 4 cod fillets (about 125-150g each)
- zest 1 lemon, then cut into wedges
- handful coriander, roughly chopped

DIRECTIONS

STEP 1

Heat the oil in a large, lidded frying pan. Cook the onion over a high heat for a few mins, then stir in the curry powder, ginger and garlic. Cook for another 1-2 mins until fragrant, then stir in the tomatoes, chickpeas and some seasoning.

STEP 2

Cook for 8-10 mins until thickened slightly, then top with the cod. Cover and cook for another 5-10 mins until the fish is cooked through. Scatter over the lemon zest and coriander, then serve with the lemon wedges to squeeze over.

LENTIL SHEPHERD'S PIE WITH CELERIAC & BUTTER BEAN MASH

Prep: 15 mins - Cook: 55 mins - Serves 4

INGREDIENTS

For the lentils

- 100g red lentils
- 2 leeks , chopped
- 4 celery sticks, chopped
- 1 reduced-salt vegetable stock cube
- 150ml red wine
- 3 heaped tbsp tomato purée
- 1 tbsp chopped thyme

For the topping

- 800g celeriac , peeled and chopped (as for cooking potatoes)
- 210g can butter beans , drained
- 50g light cream cheese
- green veg, such as broccoli , to serve (optional)

DIRECTIONS

STEP 1

Boil the celeriac until tender when tested with the point of a knife, adding the beans for the final 5 mins of cooking. Drain and roughly mash with the cream cheese until the cheese is well mixed, but the veg is still a little chunky.

STEP 2

Meanwhile, tip the lentils into a pan with the leeks, celery and stock cube. Pour in the red wine and 600ml water, and add the tomato purée and thyme. Bring to the boil, cover the pan and simmer for 20-25 mins until the lentils are soft and pulpy. Towards the end of cooking, add a splash more water if they are drying out.

STEP 3

Heat oven to 200C/180C fan/gas 6. Spoon the lentils into the base of 4 individual pie dishes, then top with the celeriac mash, smoothing it to the edge of the dishes. Bake for 35 mins until bubbling and golden, then serve with a green veg such as broccoli, if you like.

QUINOA CHILLI WITH AVOCADO & CORIANDER

Prep: 10 mins - Cook: 45 mins - Serves 2

INGREDIENTS

* 1 tbsp rapeseed oil
* 1 large onion , sliced
* 2 large garlic cloves , chopped
* 1 green pepper , chopped
* ½-1 tsp smoked paprika
* ½-1 tsp chilli powder
* 2 tsp cumin
* 2 tsp coriander
* 400g can chopped tomatoes
* ½ tsp dried oregano
* 2 tsp vegetable bouillon powder (check the label if you're vegan)
* 80g quinoa , rinsed under cold water
* 400g can black beans , drained and rinsed
* generous handful of coriander , chopped
* 2 tbsp bio yogurt or coconut yogurt (optional)
* 1 small avocado , stoned, peeled and sliced

DIRECTIONS

STEP 1

Heat the oil in a non-stick frying pan and fry the onion and garlic for 8 mins. Add the pepper and spices to taste and fry for 1 min more.

STEP 2

Tip in the tomatoes and a can of water, stir in the oregano, bouillon and quinoa, bring to the boil, then cover and simmer for 20 mins.

STEP 3

Stir in the black beans and cook, uncovered, for 5 mins more. Add most of the coriander, then serve topped with the yogurt (if using), the remaining coriander and the avocado slices.

MEATBALL & TOMATO SOUP

INGREDIENTS

- 1½ tbsp rapeseed oil
- 1 onion, finely chopped
- 2 red peppers, deseeded and sliced
- 1 garlic clove, crushed
- ½ tsp chilli flakes
- 2 x 400g cans chopped tomatoes
- 100g giant couscous
- 500ml hot vegetable stock
- 12 pork meatballs
- 150g baby spinach
- ½ small bunch of basil
- grated parmesan, to serve (optional)

DIRECTIONS

STEP 1

Heat the oil in a saucepan. Fry the onion and peppers for 7 mins, then stir through the garlic and chilli flakes and cook for 1 min. Add the tomatoes, giant couscous and veg stock and bring to a simmer.

STEP 2

Season to taste, then add the meatballs and spinach. Simmer for 5-7 mins or until cooked through. Ladle into bowls and top with the basil and some parmesan, if you like.

CURRIED CHICKEN PIE

INGREDIENTS

- 2 tbsp cold pressed rapeseed oil
- 500g chicken breasts , cut into chunks
- 4 spring onions , sliced
- 3 garlic cloves , grated
- thumb-sized piece ginger , grated
- 1 tbsp curry powder
- 1 large head broccoli , cut into florets, top of stalk thinly sliced
- 1 tsp soy sauce
- 250ml low-fat coconut milk , plus a splash

- 250ml chicken stock
- 1 heaped tsp cornflour mixed with 1 tbsp hot water
- 4 large handfuls kale
- 4 sheets filo pastry
- ½ tbsp nigella seeds

DIRECTIONS

STEP 1

Heat oven to 220C/200C fan/gas 7. Pour 1 tbsp oil into a flameproof casserole dish. Add the chicken, season and fry for 4-5 mins on a medium heat, turning, until lightly browned. Remove with tongs and set aside.

STEP 2

Pour another ½ tbsp oil into the casserole dish and add the spring onions. Fry gently for a couple of mins, then stir in the garlic, ginger and curry powder. Cook for 1 min, then tip the chicken back into the pan, along with the broccoli, soy sauce, coconut milk, chicken stock and cornflour mixture. Bring to the boil, then stir in the kale. Once the kale has wilted, take the dish off the heat.

STEP 3

Mix the remaining oil with the splash of coconut milk. Unravel the pastry. Brush each sheet lightly with the oil mixture, then scrunch up and sit on top of the pie mixture. Scatter over the nigella seeds, then cook in the oven for 12 mins, or until the pastry is a deep golden brown. Leave to stand for a couple of mins before serving.

VEGAN SHEPHERD'S PIE

Prep: 30 mins Cook: 1 hr and 20 mins Cook time is 1 hr, 45 mins if making two large pies - Serves 8 (makes eight individual or two large pies)

INGREDIENTS

- 1.2kg floury potatoes, such as Maris Piper or King Edward
- 50ml vegetable oil
- 30g dried porcini mushrooms, soaked in hot water for 15 mins, then drained (reserve the liquid)
- 2 large leeks, chopped
- 2 small onions, chopped
- 4 medium carrots (about 300g), cut into small cubes
- 1 vegetable stock cube (make sure it's vegan - we used Kallo)
- 3 garlic cloves, crushed
- 2 tbsp tomato purée

- 2 tsp smoked paprika

- 1 small butternut squash, peeled and cut into small cubes

- ½ small pack marjoram or oregano, leaves picked and roughly chopped

- ½ small pack thyme, leaves picked

- ½ small pack sage, leaves picked and roughly chopped

- 4 celery sticks, chopped

- 400g can chickpeas

- 300g frozen peas

- 300g frozen spinach

- 20ml olive oil

- small pack flat-leaf parsley, chopped

- tomato ketchup, to serve (optional)

DIRECTIONS

STEP 1

Put the unpeeled potatoes in a large saucepan, cover with water, bring to the boil and simmer for 40 mins until the skins start to split. Drain and leave to cool a little.

STEP 2

Meanwhile, heat the vegetable oil in a large heavy-based sauté pan or flameproof casserole dish. Add the mushrooms, leeks , onions, carrots and the stock cube and cook gently for 5 mins , stirring every so often. If it starts to stick, reduce the heat and stir more frequently, scraping the bits from the bottom. The veg should be soft but not mushy.

STEP 3

Add the garlic, tomato purée, paprika, squash and herbs. Stir and turn the heat up a bit, cook for 3 mins, add the celery, then stir and cook for a few more mins.

STEP 4

Tip in the chickpeas along with the water in the can and reserved mushroom stock. Add the peas and spinach and stir well. Cook for 5 mins, stirring occasionally, then season, turn off and set aside. There should still be plenty of liquid and the veg should be bright and a little firm.

STEP 5

Peel the potatoes and discard the skin. Mash 200g with a fork and stir into the veg. Break the rest of the potatoes into chunks, mix with the olive oil and parsley and season.

STEP 6

Divide the filling into the pie dishes and top with the potatotes. Heat oven to 190C/170C fan/gas 5 and bake the pies for 40-45 mins, until the top is golden and the filling is heated through. If making individual pies, check after 20 mins. Best served with tomato ketchup – as all great shepherd's pies are.

CRISPY CHILLI TURKEY NOODLES

Prep: 5 mins - Cook: 15 mins - Serves 4

INGREDIENTS

- 2 tbsp sesame oil
- 500g turkey mince
- 5cm piece ginger, grated
- 1 large garlic clove, crushed
- 3 tbsp honey
- 3 tbsp soy sauce
- 1 tbsp hot sriracha chilli sauce
- 350g dried udon noodles
- 2 limes, juiced, plus wedges to serve (optional)
- 2 large carrots, peeled and cut into matchsticks
- 4 spring onions, shredded
- 1 small bunch coriander, sliced (optional)

DIRECTIONS

STEP 1

Heat 1 tbsp oil in a large non-stick frying pan over a high heat. Once hot, add the turkey mince to the pan and fry for 10-12 mins until golden brown and crispy, breaking up the meat with a wooden spoon as you go. Add the ginger and garlic to the pan and cook for 1 min. Stir in the honey, soy and chilli sauce and cook for 2 mins.

STEP 2

Meanwhile, bring a large pan of water to the boil, add the noodles and cook following pack instructions. Drain and toss the noodles with the remaining 1 tbsp oil and all the lime juice, then divide between bowls. Top with the crispy turkey mince, carrot, onion and coriander. Serve with extra lime wedges for squeezing over, if you like.

ORZO & TOMATO SOUP

Prep: 5 mins - Cook: 25 mins - Serves 4

INGREDIENTS

* 2 tbsp olive oil

* 1 onion, chopped

* 2 celery sticks, chopped

* 2 garlic cloves, crushed

* 1 tbsp tomato purée

* 400g can chopped tomatoes

* 400g can chickpeas

* 150g orzo pasta

* 700ml vegetable stock

* 2 tbsp basil pesto

* crusty bread, to serve

DIRECTIONS

STEP 1

Heat 1 tbsp olive oil in a large saucepan. Add the onion and celery and fry for 10-15 mins, or until starting to soften, then add the garlic and cook for 1 min more. Stir in all the other ingredients, except for the pesto and remaining oil, and bring to the boil.

STEP 2

Reduce the heat and leave to simmer for 6-8 mins, or until the orzo is tender. Season to taste, then ladle into bowls.

STEP 3

Stir the remaining oil with the pesto, then drizzle over the soup. Serve with chunks of crusty bread.

CREAMY CHICKEN & ASPARAGUS BRAISE

Prep: 10 mins - Cook: 20 mins - 25 mins - Serves 2

INGREDIENTS

* 1 tbsp rapeseed oil

* 2 skinless chicken breasts (about 150g each)

* 10 medium asparagus spears , each cut into 3

* 1 large or 2 small leeks , well washed and thickly sliced

* 3 celery sticks , sliced

* 200ml reduced-salt vegetable bouillon

* 140g frozen peas

* 1 egg yolk

* 4 tbsp natural bio yogurt

- 1 garlic clove , finely grated
- ⅓ small pack fresh tarragon , chopped
- new potatoes , to serve (optional)

DIRECTIONS

STEP 1

Heat the oil in a large non-stick frying pan and fry the chicken for 5 mins, turning to brown both sides.

STEP 2

Add the asparagus (reserve the tips), leeks and celery, pour in the bouillon and simmer for 10 mins. Add the asparagus tips and peas, and cook for 5 mins more.

STEP 3

Meanwhile, stir the egg yolk with the yogurt and garlic. Stir the yogurt mixture into the vegetables and add the tarragon. Divide between two warm plates, then place the chicken on top of the vegetables. Serve with new potatoes, if you like.

LOW-FAT CHICKEN BIRYANI

Prep: 25 mins - Cook: 1 hr and 35 mins Plus marinating - Serves 5

INGREDIENTS

- 3 garlic cloves , finely grated
- 2 tsp finely grated ginger
- ¼ tsp ground cinnamon
- 1 tsp turmeric
- 5 tbsp natural yogurt
- 600g boneless, skinless chicken breast , cut into 4-5cm pieces
- 2 tbsp semi-skimmed milk
- good pinch saffron
- 4 medium onions
- 4 tbsp rapeseed oil
- ½ tsp hot chilli powder
- 1 cinnamon stick , broken in half
- 5 green cardamom pods , lightly bashed to split
- 3 cloves
- 1 tsp cumin seed
- 280g basmati rice
- 700ml chicken stock

- 1 tsp garam masala
- handful chopped coriander leaves

DIRECTIONS

STEP 1

In a mixing bowl, stir together the garlic, ginger, cinnamon, turmeric and yogurt with some pepper and ¼ tsp salt. Tip in the chicken pieces and stir to coat (see step 1, above). Cover and marinate in the fridge for about 1 hr or longer if you have time. Warm the milk to tepid, stir in the saffron and set aside.

STEP 2

Heat oven to 200C/180C fan/gas 6. Slice each onion in half lengthways, reserve half and cut the other half into thin slices. Pour 1½ tbsp of the oil onto a baking tray, scatter over the sliced onion, toss to coat, then spread out in a thin, even layer (step 2). Roast for 40-45 mins, stirring halfway, until golden.

STEP 3

When the chicken has marinated, thinly slice the reserved onion. Heat 1 tbsp oil in a large sauté or frying pan. Fry the onion for 4-5 mins until golden. Stir in the chicken, a spoonful at a time, frying until it is no longer opaque, before adding the next spoonful (this helps to prevent the yogurt from curdling). Once the last of the chicken has been added, stir-fry for a further 5 mins until everything looks juicy. Scrape any sticky bits off the bottom of the pan, stir in the chilli powder, then pour in 100ml water, cover and simmer on a low heat for 15 mins. Remove and set aside.

STEP 4

Cook the rice while the chicken simmers. Heat another 1 tbsp oil in a large sauté pan, then drop in the cinnamon stick, cardamom, cloves and cumin seeds. Fry briefly until their aroma is released. Tip in the rice (step 3) and fry for 1 min, stirring constantly. Stir in the stock and bring to the boil. Lower the heat and simmer, covered, for about 8 mins or until all the stock has been absorbed. Remove from the heat and leave with the lid on for a few mins, so the rice can fluff up. Stir the garam masala into the remaining 1½ tsp oil and set aside. When the onions are roasted, remove and reduce oven to 180C/160C fan/gas 4.

STEP 5

Spoon half the chicken and its juices into an ovenproof dish, about 25 x 18 x 6cm, then scatter over a third of the roasted onions. Remove the whole spices from the rice, then layer half of the rice over the chicken and onions. Drizzle over the spiced oil. Spoon over the rest of the chicken and a third more onions. Top with the remaining rice (step 4) and drizzle over the saffron-infused milk. Scatter over the rest of the onions, cover tightly with foil and heat through in the oven for about 25 mins. Serve scattered with the mint and coriander.

SLOW COOKER SHEPHERD'S PIE

Prep: 1 hr - Cook: 5 hrs - Serves 4

INGREDIENTS

- 1 tbsp olive oil
- 1 onion, finely chopped
- 3-4 thyme sprigs
- 2 carrots, finely diced
- 250g lean (10%) mince lamb or beef
- 1 tbsp plain flour
- 1 tbsp tomato purée
- 400g can lentils, or white beans
- 1 tsp Worcestershire sauce

For the topping

- 650g potatoes, peeled and cut into chunks
- 250g sweet potatoes, peeled and cut into chunks
- 2 tbsp half-fat crème fraîche

DIRECTIONS

STEP 1

Heat the slow cooker if necessary. Heat the oil in a large frying pan. Tip the onions and thyme sprigs and fry for 2-3 mins. Then add the carrots and fry together, stirring occasionally until the vegetables start to brown. Stir in the mince and fry for 1-2 mins until no longer pink. Stir in the flour then cook for another 1-2 mins. Stir in the tomato purée and lentils and season with pepper and the Worcestershire sauce, adding a splash of water if you think the mixture is too dry. Scrape everything into the slow cooker.

STEP 2

Meanwhile cook both lots of potatoes in simmering water for 12-13 minutes or until they are cooked through. Drain well and then mash with the crème fraîche. Spoon this on top of the mince mixture and cook on Low for 5 hours - the mixture should be bubbling at the sides when it is ready. Crisp up the potato topping under the grill if you like.

HOME-STYLE PORK CURRY WITH CAULIFLOWER RICE

Prep: 15 mins - Cook: 1 hr - Serves 4

INGREDIENTS

For the curry

- 425g lean pork fillet (tenderloin), cubed

- 2 tbsp Madras curry powder

- 2 tbsp red wine vinegar

- 1 tbsp rapeseed oil

- 1 large onion , finely chopped

- 2 tbsp finely shredded ginger

- 1 tsp fennel , toasted in a pan then crushed

- 1 tsp cumin , toasted in a pan then crushed

- 400g can chopped tomatoes

- 2 tbsp red lentils

- 350g pack baby aubergine , quartered

- 1 reduced-salt vegetable stock cube

For the cauliflower rice

- 1 medium cauliflower

- good handful coriander , chopped

- cumin seeds , toasted (optional)

DIRECTIONS

STEP 1

Tip the pork into a bowl and stir in the curry powder and vinegar. Set aside. Heat the oil in a heavy-based pan and fry the onion and ginger for 10 mins, stirring frequently, until golden. Tip in the pork mixture and fry for a few mins more. Remove the pork and set aside. Stir in the toasted spices, then tip in the tomatoes, lentils and aubergine, and crumble in the stock cube. Cover and leave to simmer for 40 mins, stirring frequently, until the aubergine is almost cooked. If it starts to look dry, add a splash of water. Return the pork to the pan and cook for a further 10-20 mins until the pork is cooked and tender.

STEP 2

Just before serving, cut the hard core and stalks from the cauliflower and pulse the rest in a food processor to make grains the size of rice. Tip into a heatproof bowl, cover with cling film, then pierce and microwave for 7 mins on High – there is no need to add any water. Stir in the coriander and serve with the curry. For spicier rice, add some toasted cumin seeds.

MINTY GRIDDLED CHICKEN & PEACH SALAD

Prep: 10 mins - Cook: 15 mins |Serves 2

INGREDIENTS

- 1 lime , zested and juiced
- 1 tbsp rapeseed oil
- 2 tbsp mint , finely chopped, plus a few leaves to serve
- 1 garlic clove , finely grated
- 2 skinless chicken breast fillets (300g)
- 160g fine beans , trimmed and halved
- 2 peaches (200g), each cut into 8 thick wedges
- 1 red onion , cut into wedges
- 1 large Little Gem lettuce (165g), roughly shredded
- ½ x 60g pack rocket
- 1 small avocado , stoned and sliced
- 240g cooked new potatoes

DIRECTIONS

STEP 1

Mix the lime zest and juice, oil and mint, then put half in a bowl with the garlic. Thickly slice the chicken at a slight angle, add to the garlic mixture and toss together with plenty of black pepper.

STEP 2

Cook the beans in a pan of water for 3-4 mins until just tender. Meanwhile, griddle the chicken and onion for a few mins each side until cooked and tender. Transfer to a plate, then quickly griddle the peaches. If you don't have a griddle pan, use a non-stick frying pan with a drop of oil.

STEP 3

Toss the warm beans and onion in the remaining mint mixture, and pile onto a platter or into individual shallow bowls with the lettuce and rocket. Top with the avocado, peaches and chicken and scatter over the mint. Serve with the potatoes while still warm.

PARMA PORK WITH POTATO SALAD

Prep: 15 mins - Cook: 15 mins - Serves 2

INGREDIENTS

- 175g new potatoes (we used Jersey Royals), scrubbed and thickly sliced
- 3 celery sticks, thickly sliced
- 3 tbsp bio yogurt
- 2 gherkins (about 85g each), sliced
- ¼ tsp caraway seeds
- ½ tsp Dijon mustard

- 2 x 100g pieces lean pork tenderloin
- 2 tsp chopped sage
- 2 slices Parma ham
- 1 tsp rapeseed oil
- 2 tsp balsamic vinegar
- 2 handfuls salad leaves

DIRECTIONS

STEP 1

Bring a pan of water to the boil, add the potatoes and celery and cook for 8 mins. Meanwhile, mix the yogurt, guerkins, caraway and mustard in a bowl. When the potatoes and celery are cooked, drain and set aside for a few mins to cool a little.

STEP 2

Bash the pork pieces with a rolling pin to flatten them. Sprinkle over the sage and some pepper, then top each with a slice of Parma ham. Heat the oil in a non-stick pan, add the pork and cook for a couple of mins each side, turning carefully. Add the balsamic vinegar and let it sizzle in the pan.

STEP 3

Stir the potatoes and celery into the dressing and serve with the pork, with some salad leaves on the side.

YAKI UDON

Prep: 10 mins - Cook: 5 mins - Serves 2

INGREDIENTS

- 250g dried udon noodles (400g frozen or fresh)
- 2 tbsp sesame oil
- 1 onion, thickly sliced
- ¼ head white cabbage, roughly sliced
- 10 shiitake mushrooms
- 4 spring onions, finely sliced

For the sauce

- 4 tbsp mirin
- 2 tbsp soy sauce
- 1 tbsp caster sugar
- 1 tbsp Worcestershire sauce (or vegetarian alternative)

DIRECTIONS

STEP 1

Boil some water in a large saucepan. Add 250ml cold water and the udon noodles. (As they are so thick, adding cold water helps them to cook a little bit slower so the middle cooks through). If using frozen or fresh noodles, cook for 2 mins or until al dente; dried will take longer, about 5-6 mins. Drain and leave in the colander.

STEP 2

Heat 1 tbsp of the oil, add the onion and cabbage and sauté for 5 mins until softened. Add the mushrooms and some spring onions, and sauté for 1 more min. Pour in the remaining sesame oil and the noodles. If using cold noodles, let them heat through before adding the ingredients for the sauce – otherwise tip in straight away and keep stir-frying until sticky and piping hot. Sprinkle with the remaining spring onions.

SESAME SALMON, PURPLE SPROUTING BROCCOLI & SWEET POTATO MASH

Prep: 10 mins - Cook: 15 mins - Serves 2

INGREDIENTS

- 1 ½ tbsp sesame oil
- 1 tbsp low-salt soy sauce
- thumb-sized piece ginger, grated
- 1 garlic clove, crushed
- 1 tsp honey
- 2 sweet potatoes, scrubbed and cut into wedges
- 1 lime, cut into wedges
- 2 boneless skinless salmon fillets
- 250g purple sprouting broccoli
- 1 tbsp sesame seeds
- 1 red chilli, thinly sliced (deseeded if you don't like it too hot)

DIRECTIONS

STEP 1

Heat oven to 200C/180 fan/ gas 6 and line a baking tray with parchment. Mix together 1/2 tbsp sesame oil, the soy, ginger, garlic and honey. Put the sweet potato wedges, skin and all, into a glass bowl with the lime wedges. Cover with cling film and microwave on high for 12-14 mins until completely soft.

STEP 2

Meanwhile, spread the broccoli and salmon out on the baking tray. Spoon over the marinade and season. Roast in the oven for 10-12 mins, then sprinkle over the sesame seeds.

STEP 3

Remove the lime wedges and roughly mash the sweet potato using a fork. Mix in the remaining sesame oil, the chilli and some seasoning. Divide between plates, along with the salmon and broccoli.

LIGHTER CHICKEN CACCIATORE

Prep: 15 mins - Cook: 50 mins - Serves 4

INGREDIENTS

- 1 tbsp olive oil
- 3 slices prosciutto, fat removed, chopped
- 1 medium onion, chopped
- 2 garlic cloves, finely chopped
- 2 sage sprigs
- 2 rosemary sprigs
- 4 skinless chicken breasts (550g total weight), preferably organic
- 150ml dry white wine
- 400g can plum tomatoes in natural juice
- 1 tbsp tomato purée
- 225g chestnut mushrooms, quartered or halved if large
- small handful chopped flat-leaf parsley, to serve

DIRECTIONS

STEP 1

Heat the oil in a large non-stick frying pan. Tip in the prosciutto and fry for about 2 mins until crisp. Remove with a slotted spoon, letting any fat drain back into the pan, and set aside. Put the onion, garlic and herbs in the pan and fry for 3-4 mins.

STEP 2

Spread the onion out in the pan, then lay the chicken breasts on top. Season with pepper and fry for 5 mins over a medium heat, turning the chicken once, until starting to brown on both sides and the onion is caramelising on the bottom of the pan. Remove the chicken and set aside on a plate. Raise the heat, give it a quick stir and, when sizzling, pour in the wine and let it bubble for 2 mins to reduce slightly.

STEP 3

Lower the heat to medium, return the prosciutto to the pan, then stir in the tomatoes (breaking them up with your spoon), tomato purée and mushrooms. Spoon 4 tbsp of water into the empty tomato can, swirl it around, then pour it into the pan. Cover and simmer for 15-20 mins or until the sauce has thickened and reduced slightly, then return the chicken to the pan and cook, uncovered, for about 15 mins or until the chicken is cooked through. Season and scatter over the parsley to serve.

BALSAMIC BEEF WITH BEETROOT & ROCKET

Prep: 15 mins - Cook: 25 mins - Serves 2

INGREDIENTS

- 240g beef sirloin , fat trimmed
- 1 tbsp balsamic vinegar
- 2 tsp thyme leaves
- 2 garlic cloves , 1 finely grated, 1 sliced
- 2 tsp rapeseed oil
- 2 red onions , halved and sliced
- 175g fine beans , trimmed
- 2 cooked beetroot , halved and cut into wedges
- 6 pitted Kalamata olives , quartered
- 2 handfuls rocket

DIRECTIONS

STEP 1

Beat the steak with a rolling pin until it is about the thickness of two £1 coins, then cut into two equal pieces. In a bowl, mix the balsamic, thyme, grated garlic, half the oil and a grinding of black pepper. Place the steaks in the marinade and set aside.

STEP 2

Heat the remaining 1 tsp oil in a large non-stick frying pan, and fry the onions and garlic for 8-10 mins, stirring frequently, until soft and starting to brown. Meanwhile, steam the beans for 4-6 mins or until just tender.

STEP 3

Push the onion mixture to one side in the pan. Lift the steaks from the bowl, shake off any excess marinade, and sear in the pan for 2½-3 mins, turning once, until cooked but still a little pink inside. Pile the beans onto plates and place the steaks on top. Add the beetroot wedges, olives and remaining marinade to the pan and cook briefly to heat through, then spoon on top and around the steaks. Add the rocket and serve.

CHARRED SPRING ONIONS & TERIYAKI TOFU

Prep: 5 mins - Cook: 25 mins - Serves 2

INGREDIENTS

- 150g wholegrain rice
- 50ml soy sauce
- 2 tbsp mirin
- ½ tsp grated ginger
- 1 tsp honey
- 350g firm tofu (we used Cauldron)
- 1 bunch spring onions , ends trimmed
- 2 tsp sunflower oil
- ½ tsp sesame seeds
- 1 red chilli , sliced (optional)

DIRECTIONS

STEP 1

Cook the rice according to pack instructions. Pour the soy sauce, mirin, ginger and honey into a small saucepan and add 50ml water. Bring to a simmer and cook for around 5 mins or until slightly thickened. Remove from the heat and set aside until needed.

STEP 2

If your tofu doesn't feel very firm, you'll need to press it. To do this, wrap the block of tofu in a few layers of kitchen paper, then weigh it down with a heavy pan or tray for 10-15 mins – the longer you press it, the firmer it will be. Cut the tofu into thick slices.

STEP 3

Heat a griddle pan over high heat and lightly brush the tofu and spring onions with the oil. Griddle the tofu and spring onion until deep char lines appear on both sides (around 4 mins each side) – you may have to do this in batches depending on the size of your griddle pan.

STEP 4

Divide the cooked rice between two plates, top with the tofu and spring onion, then drizzle with the teriyaki sauce. Garnish with the sesame seeds and sliced red chilli, if using.

SESAME CHICKEN & PRAWN SKEWERS

Prep: 15 mins - Cook: 5 mins Plus marinating - Makes 20

INGREDIENTS

- thumb-sized piece ginger , grated
- 1 large garlic clove , grated
- 1 tsp honey
- 1½ tsp soy sauce
- 1 tsp sesame oil
- ½ lime , juiced
- 1 tbsp sesame seeds
- 1 skinless chicken breast , cut into 10 pieces
- 10 raw king prawns
- 1 broccoli head , cut into 20 florets
- 20 cocktail skewers

DIRECTIONS

STEP 1

Combine the ginger, garlic, honey, soy sauce, sesame oil, lime juice and sesame seeds. Divide between two bowls, then add the chicken pieces to one and the prawns to the other. Toss both mixtures well, then leave to marinate in the fridge for 15 mins.

STEP 2

Cook the chicken in a frying pan over a medium-high heat for 3 mins, then push to one side and add the prawns to the other side of the pan. Cook for 2 mins until the prawns are pink and the chicken is cooked through (use two separate pans if anyone you're cooking for has an allergy or is a pescatarian). Put the broccoli in a microwaveable bowl with a splash of water, then cover and cook on high for 5 mins.

STEP 3

Thread half of the skewers with chicken and broccoli and the other half with prawns and broccoli.

CHIPOTLE CHICKEN TACOS WITH PINEAPPLE SALSA

Prep: 10 mins - Cook: 10 mins - Serves 4

INGREDIENTS

- 500g skinless boneless chicken thighs
- 1 tbsp vegetable oil
- 1 medium onion , chopped

- 2 tsp sweet smoked paprika
- 2 tsp ground cumin
- 2 tbsp cider vinegar
- 1 tbsp chipotle paste
- 200ml passata
- 2 tbsp soft brown sugar
- ½ small pineapple , cored, peeled and chopped
- ½ small pack coriander , chopped
- corn or flour tortillas
- hot sauce (I like Tabasco Chipotle), to serve

DIRECTIONS

STEP 1

In a food processor, roughly blitz the chicken thighs into chunky mince. Alternatively, chop into bite-sized pieces.

STEP 2

Heat the oil in a large saucepan. Add half the onion and the chicken mince. Season well and cook for about 5 mins on a high heat to brown, breaking up the meat with a spoon. Add the spices, vinegar, chipotle paste, passata and sugar. Cook for another 5 mins, then remove from the heat.

STEP 3

In a small bowl, mix the remaining onion, the pineapple and coriander. Serve the chicken and the pineapple salsa with warm tortillas and hot sauce.

COD PUTTANESCA WITH SPINACH & SPAGHETTI

Prep: 10 mins - Cook: 17 mins - Serves 2

INGREDIENTS

- 100g wholemeal spaghetti
- 1 large onion , sliced
- 1 tbsp rapeseed oil
- 1 red chilli , deseeded and sliced
- 2 garlic cloves , chopped
- 200g cherry tomatoes , halved
- 1 tsp cider vinegar

- 2 tsp capers

- 5 Kalamata olives , halved

- ½ tsp smoked paprika

- 2 skinless cod fillet or loins

- 160g spinach leaves

- small handful chopped parsley , to serve

DIRECTIONS

STEP 1

Boil the spaghetti for 10 mins until al dente, adding the spinach for the last 2 mins. Meanwhile, fry the onion in the oil in a large non-stick frying pan with a lid until tender and turning golden. Stir in the chilli and garlic, then add the tomatoes.

STEP 2

Add the vinegar, capers, olives and paprika with a ladleful of the pasta water. Put the cod fillets on top, then cover the pan and cook for 5-7 mins until the fish just flakes. Drain the pasta and wilted spinach and pile on to plates, then top with the fish and sauce. Sprinkle over some parsley to serve.

BASIC LENTILS

Prep: 10 mins - Cook: 45 mins - Makes 6 portions

INGREDIENTS

- 2 tbsp coconut oil

- 2 onions , chopped

- 4 garlic cloves , chopped

- large piece of ginger , chopped

- 300g red split lentils

- 1 tsp turmeric

- 2 tomatoes , roughly chopped

- 1 tsp coriander seeds

- 1 tsp cumin seeds

- 1 tsp black mustard seeds

- 1 lemon , juiced

DIRECTIONS

STEP 1

Melt 1 tbsp coconut oil in a large saucepan. Add the onion and a pinch of salt, and cook for 8 mins. Stir in the garlic and ginger and cook for a few mins more. Add the lentils, turmeric and tomatoes, stir to combine, then pour in 1 litre of water. Bring to the boil, then turn down and simmer for 25-30 mins, stirring occasionally, until the lentils are tender.

STEP 2

Heat the rest of the oil in a frying pan. When it's very hot, add the spices and fry for a min or so until fragrant, then stir them through. Add the lemon juice and season to taste. Will keep for four days in the fridge, or freeze it in batches and use to make our lentil kedgeree, lentil fritters, or spinach dhal with harissa yogurt.

BASIC LENTILS

Prep: 10 mins - Cook: 45 mins - Makes 6 portions

INGREDIENTS

- 2 tbsp coconut oil
- 2 onions , chopped
- 4 garlic cloves , chopped
- large piece of ginger , chopped
- 300g red split lentils
- 1 tsp turmeric
- 2 tomatoes , roughly chopped
- 1 tsp coriander seeds
- 1 tsp cumin seeds
- 1 tsp black mustard seeds
- 1 lemon , juiced

DIRECTIONS

STEP 1

Melt 1 tbsp coconut oil in a large saucepan. Add the onion and a pinch of salt, and cook for 8 mins. Stir in the garlic and ginger and cook for a few mins more. Add the lentils, turmeric and tomatoes, stir to combine, then pour in 1 litre of water. Bring to the boil, then turn down and simmer for 25-30 mins, stirring occasionally, until the lentils are tender.

STEP 2

Heat the rest of the oil in a frying pan. When it's very hot, add the spices and fry for a min or so until fragrant, then stir them through. Add the lemon juice and season to taste. Will keep for four days in the fridge, or freeze it in batches and use to make our lentil kedgeree, lentil fritters, or spinach dhal with harissa yogurt.

CHICKEN & MUSHROOM PANCAKE TOPPING

Prep: 5 mins - Cook: 15 mins - Serves 4

INGREDIENTS

- a large knob of butter
- 250g chopped chestnut mushrooms
- 1 crushed garlic clove
- 2 tbsp flour
- 250ml milk
- 2 tsp Dijon mustard
- 2 tbsp mushroom ketchup
- 2 cooked chicken breasts
- a handful chopped parsley

DIRECTIONS

STEP 1

Melt the butter in a pan, add the mushrooms and cook until softened, about 8 mins. Add the garlic and cook for 1 min more, then stir in the flour, milk, mustard and ketchup. Stir for a few mins until you have a thick sauce, then season well.

STEP 2

Shred the chicken and add to the sauce along with the parsley. Top four warm pancakes (see our easy pancakes recipe) with the chicken & mushroom mix and serve.

BANANA PANCAKES

Prep: 5 mins Cook: 5 mins - Serves 2 (makes 4)

INGREDIENTS

- 1 large banana
- 2 medium eggs, beaten
- pinch of baking powder (gluten-free if coeliac)
- splash of vanilla extract
- 1 tsp oil
- 25g pecans, roughly chopped

- 125g raspberries

DIRECTIONS

STEP 1

In a bowl, mash 1 large banana with a fork until it resembles a thick purée.

STEP 2

Stir in 2 beaten eggs, a pinch of baking powder (gluten-free if coeliac) and a splash of vanilla extract.

STEP 3

Heat a large non-stick frying pan or pancake pan over a medium heat and brush with ½ tsp oil.

STEP 4

Using half the batter, spoon two pancakes into the pan, cook for 1-2 mins each side, then tip onto a plate. Repeat the process with another ½ tsp oil and the remaining batter.

STEP 5

Top the pancakes with 25g roughly chopped pecans and 125g raspberries.

LAMB & SQUASH BIRYANI WITH CUCUMBER RAITA

Prep: 10 mins - Cook: 25 mins - Serves 4

INGREDIENTS

- 4 lean lamb steaks (about 400g), trimmed of all fat, cut into chunks
- 2 garlic cloves , finely grated
- 8 tsp chopped fresh ginger
- 3 tsp ground coriander
- 4 tsp rapeseed oil
- 4 onions , sliced
- 2 red chillies , deseeded and chopped
- 170g brown basmati rice
- 320g diced butternut squash
- 2 tsp cumin seeds
- 2 tsp vegetable bouillon powder
- 20cm length cucumber , grated
- 100ml bio yogurt
- 4 tbsp chopped mint , plus a few extra leaves
- handful coriander , chopped

DIRECTIONS

STEP 1

Mix the lamb with the garlic, 2 tsp chopped ginger and 1 tsp ground coriander and set aside.

STEP 2

Heat 2 tsp oil in a non-stick pan. Add the onions, the remaining ginger and chilli and stir-fry briefly over a high heat so they start to soften. Add the rice and squash and stir over the heat for a few mins. Tip in all the remaining spices, then stir in 500ml boiling water and the bouillon. Cover the pan and simmer for 20 mins.

STEP 3

Meanwhile, mix the cucumber, yogurt and mint together in a bowl to make a raita. Chill half for later.

STEP 4

About 5 mins before the rice is ready, heat the remaining oil in a non-stick frying pan, add the lamb and stir for a few mins until browned but still nice tender. Toss into the spiced rice with the coriander and serve with the raita and a few mint or coriander leaves on top.

ROASTED RED PEPPER & TOMATO SOUP WITH RICOTTA

Prep: 10 mins - Cook: 30 mins - Serves 2

INGREDIENTS

- 400g tomatoes , halved
- 1 red onion , quartered
- 2 Romano peppers , roughly chopped
- 2 tbsp good quality olive oil
- 2 garlic cloves , bashed in their skins
- few thyme sprigs
- 1 tbsp red wine vinegar
- 2 tbsp ricotta
- few basil leaves
- 1 tbsp mixed seeds , toasted
- bread , to serve

DIRECTIONS

STEP 1

Heat oven to 200C/180C fan/gas 6. Put the tomatoes, onion and peppers in a roasting tin, toss with the oil and season. Nestle in the garlic and thyme sprigs, then roast for 25-30 mins until all the veg has softened and slightly caramelised. Squeeze the garlic cloves out of their skins into the tin, strip the leaves off the thyme and discard the stalks and garlic skins. Mix the vinegar into the tin then blend everything in a bullet blender or using a stick blender, adding enough water to loosen to your preferred consistency (we used around 150ml).

STEP 2

Reheat the soup if necessary, taste for seasoning, then spoon into two bowls and top each with a spoonful of ricotta, a few basil leaves, the seeds and a drizzle of oil. Serve with bread for dunking.

CHUNKY VEGETABLE & BROWN RICE SOUP

Prep: 18 mins - Cook: 50 mins - Serves 4

INGREDIENTS

- 2 tbsp cold-pressed rapeseed oil
- 1 medium onion , halved and sliced
- 2 garlic cloves , finely sliced
- 2 celery sticks , trimmed and thinly sliced
- 2medium carrots , cut into chunks
- 2 medium parsnips , cut into chunks
- 1 tbsp finely chopped thyme leaves
- 100g wholegrain rice
- 2medium leeks , sliced
- ½ small pack parsley , to garnish

DIRECTIONS

STEP 1

Heat the oil in a large non-stick pan and add the onion, garlic, celery, carrots, parsnips and thyme. Cover with a lid and cook gently for 15 mins, stirring occasionally, until the onions are softened and beginning to colour. Add the rice and pour in 1.2 litres cold water. Bring to the boil, then reduce the heat to a simmer and cook, uncovered, for 15 mins, stirring occasionally.

STEP 2

Season the soup with plenty of ground black pepper and salt to taste, then stir in the leeks. Return to a gentle simmer and cook for a further 5 mins or until the leeks have softened. Adjust the seasoning to taste and blitz half the soup with a stick blender, leaving the other half chunky, if you like. Top with the parsley and serve in deep bowls.

SALMON SALAD WITH SESAME DRESSING

Prep: 7 mins - Cook: 16 mins - Serves 2

INGREDIENTS

For the salad

- 250g new potatoes , sliced
- 160g French beans , trimmed
- 2 wild salmon fillets
- 80g salad leaves
- 4 small clementines , 3 sliced, 1 juiced
- handful of basil , chopped
- handful of coriander , chopped

For the dressing

- 2 tsp sesame oil
- 2 tsp tamari
- ½ lemon , juiced
- 1 red chilli , deseeded and chopped
- 2 tbsp finely chopped onion (1/4 small onion)

DIRECTIONS

STEP 1

Steam the potatoes and beans in a steamer basket set over a pan of boiling water for 8 mins. Arrange the salmon fillets on top and steam for a further 6-8 mins, or until the salmon flakes easily when tested with a fork.

STEP 2

Meanwhile, mix the dressing ingredients together along with the clementine juice. If eating straightaway, divide the salad leaves between two plates and top with the warm potatoes and beans and the clementine slices. Arrange the salmon fillets on top, scatter over the herbs and spoon over the dressing. If taking to work, prepare the potatoes, beans and salmon the night before, then pack into a rigid airtight container with the salad leaves kept separate. Put the salad elements together and dress just before eating to prevent the leaves from wilting.

GINGER CHICKEN & GREEN BEAN NOODLES

INGREDIENTS

- ½ tbsp vegetable oil
- 2 skinless chicken breasts, sliced
- 200g green beans , trimmed and halved crosswise
- thumb-sized piece of ginger , peeled and cut into matchsticks
- 2 garlic cloves , sliced
- 1 ball stem ginger , finely sliced, plus 1 tsp syrup from the jar
- 1 tsp cornflour , mixed with 1 tbsp water
- 1 tsp dark soy sauce , plus extra to serve (optional)
- 2 tsp rice vinegar
- 200g cooked egg noodles

DIRECTIONS

STEP 1

Heat the oil in a wok over a high heat and stir-fry the chicken for 5 mins. Add the green beans and stir-fry for 4-5 mins more until the green beans are just tender, and the chicken is just cooked through.

STEP 2

Stir in the fresh ginger and garlic, and stir-fry for 2 mins, then add the stem ginger and syrup, the cornflour mix, soy sauce and vinegar. Stir-fry for 1 min, then toss in the noodles. Cook until everything is hot and the sauce coats the noodles. Drizzle with more soy, if you like, and serve.

POTATO, PEA & EGG CURRY ROTIS

Prep: 5 mins - Cook: 25 mins - Serves 4

INGREDIENTS

- 1 tbsp oil
- 2 tbsp mild curry paste
- 400g can chopped tomatoes
- 2 potatoes , cut into small chunks
- 200g peas
- 3 eggs , hard-boiled
- pack rotis , warmed through
- 150g tub natural yogurt , to serve

DIRECTIONS

STEP 1

Heat the oil in a saucepan and briefly fry the curry paste. Tip in the tomatoes and half a can of water and bring to a simmer. Add the potatoes and cook for 20 mins, or until the potato is tender. Stir in the peas and cook for 3 mins.

STEP 2

Halve the eggs and place them on top of the curry, then warm everything through. Serve with the rotis and yogurt on the side.

THAI PRAWN & GINGER NOODLES

Prep: 15 mins - Cook: 15 mins plus soaking - Serves 2

INGREDIENTS

- 100g folded rice noodles (sen lek)
- zest and juice 1 small orange
- 1½-2 tbsp red curry paste
- 1-2 tsp fish sauce
- 2 tsp light brown soft sugar
- 1 tbsp sunflower oil
- 25g ginger, scraped and shredded
- 2 large garlic cloves, sliced
- 1 red pepper, deseeded and sliced
- 85g sugar snap peas, halved lengthways
- 140g beansprouts
- 175g pack raw king prawns
- handful chopped basil
- handful chopped coriander

DIRECTIONS

STEP 1

Put the noodles in a bowl and pour over boiling water to cover them. Set aside to soak for 10 mins. Stir together the orange juice and zest, curry paste, fish sauce, sugar and 3 tbsp water to make a sauce.

STEP 2

Heat the oil in a large wok and add half the ginger and the garlic. Cook, stirring, for 1 min. Add the pepper and stir-fry for 3 mins more. Toss in the sugar snaps, cook briefly, then pour in the curry sauce. Add the beansprouts and prawns, and continue cooking until the prawns just turn pink. Drain the noodles, then toss these into the pan with the herbs and remaining ginger. Mix until the noodles are well coated in the sauce, then serve.

EASY SOUP MAKER LENTIL SOUP

Prep: 5 mins - Cook: 30 mins - Serves 4

INGREDIENTS

- 750ml vegetable or ham stock
- 75g red lentils
- 3 carrots , finely chopped
- 1 medium leek , sliced (150g)
- small handful chopped parsley , to serve

DIRECTIONS

STEP 1

Put the stock, lentils, carrots and leek into a soup maker, and press the 'chunky soup' function. Make sure you don't fill it above the max fill line. The soup will look a little foamy to start, but don't worry – it will disappear once cooked.

STEP 2

Once the cycle is complete, check the lentils are tender, and season well. Scatter over the parsley to serve.

RASPBERRY TEA ICE LOLLIES

Prep: 10 mins plus 4 hrs freezing - Serves 6

INGREDIENTS

- 100g raspberries
- 3 raspberry teabag
- 1 tbsp maple syrup
- juice of 1 lime

DIRECTIONS

STEP 1

Put the raspberries, raspberry tea bags and maple syrup in a bowl, then pour over 350ml boiling water.

Leave to infuse for 10 mins, then remove the tea bags, stir in the lime juice and leave to cool.

CABBAGE SOUP

Prep: 20 mins - Cook: 50 mins - Serves 6

INGREDIENTS

- 2 tbsp olive oil
- 1 large onion , finely chopped

- 2 celery sticks , finely chopped
- 1 large carrot , finely chopped
- 70g smoked pancetta , diced (optional)
- 1 large Savoy cabbage , shredded
- 2 fat garlic cloves , crushed
- 1 heaped tsp sweet smoked paprika
- 1 tbsp finely chopped rosemary
- 1 x 400g can chopped tomatoes
- 1.7l hot vegetable stock
- 1 x 400g can chickpeas , drained and rinsed
- shaved parmesan (or vegetarian alternative), to serve (optional)
- crusty bread , to serve (optional)

DIRECTIONS

STEP 1

Heat the oil in a casserole pot over a low heat. Add the onion, celery and carrot, along with a generous pinch of salt, and fry gently for 15 mins, or until the veg begins to soften. If you're using pancetta, add it to the pan, turn up the heat and fry for a few mins more until turning golden brown. Tip in the cabbage and fry for 5 mins, then stir through the garlic, paprika and rosemary and cook for 1 min more.

STEP 2

Tip the chopped tomatoes and stock into the pan. Bring to a simmer, then cook, uncovered, for 30 mins, adding the chickpeas for the final 10 mins. Season generously with salt and black pepper.

STEP 3

Ladle the soup into six deep bowls. Serve with the shaved parmesan and crusty bread, if you like.

RED PEPPER, SQUASH & HARISSA SOUP

Prep: 15 mins - Cook: 1 hr - Serves 6

INGREDIENTS

- 1 small butternut squash (about 600-700g), peeled and cut into chunks
- 2 red pepper , roughly chopped
- 2 red onion , roughly chopped
- 3 tbsp rapeseed oil
- 3 garlic cloves in their skins
- 1 tbsp ground coriander
- 2 tsp ground cumin

- 1.2l chicken or vegetable stock
- 2 tbsp harissa paste
- 50ml double cream

DIRECTIONS

STEP 1

Heat oven to 180C/160C fan/gas 4. Put all the veg on a large baking tray and toss together with rapeseed oil, garlic cloves in their skins, ground coriander, ground cumin and some seasoning. Roast for 45 mins, moving the veg around in the tray after 30 mins, until soft and starting to caramelise. Squeeze the garlic cloves out of their skins. Tip everything into a large pan. Add the chicken or vegetable stock, harissa paste and double cream. Bring to a simmer and bubble for a few mins. Blitz the soup in a blender, check the seasoning and add more liquid if you need to. Serve swirled with extra cream and harissa.

LINGUINE WITH AVOCADO, TOMATO & LIME

Prep: 20 mins - Cook: 10 mins - Serves 2

INGREDIENTS

- 115g wholemeal linguine
- 1 lime, zested and juiced
- 1 avocado, stoned, peeled, and chopped
- 2 large ripe tomatoes, chopped
- ½ pack fresh coriander, chopped
- 1 red onion, finely chopped
- 1 red chilli, deseeded and finely chopped (optional)

DIRECTIONS

STEP 1

Cook the pasta according to pack instructions – about 10 mins. Meanwhile, put the lime juice and zest in a medium bowl with the avocado, tomatoes, coriander, onion and chilli, if using, and mix well.

STEP 2

Drain the pasta, toss into the bowl and mix well. Serve straight away while still warm, or cold.

ROASTED ROOTS & SAGE SOUP

Prep: 15 mins - Cook: 45 mins - Serves 2

INGREDIENTS

- 1 parsnip , peeled and chopped
- 2 carrots , peeled and chopped
- 300g turnip , swede or celeriac, chopped
- 4 garlic cloves , skin left on
- 1 tbsp rapeseed oil , plus ½ tsp
- 1 tsp maple syrup
- ¼ small bunch of sage , leaves picked, 4 whole, the rest finely chopped
- 750ml vegetable stock
- grating of nutmeg
- 1½ tbsp fat-free yogurt

DIRECTIONS

STEP 1

Heat the oven to 200C/180C fan/gas 6. Toss the root vegetables and garlic with 1 tbsp oil and season. Tip onto a baking tray and roast for 30 mins until tender. Toss with the maple syrup and the chopped sage, then roast for another 10 mins until golden and glazed. Brush the whole sage leaves with ½ tsp oil and add to the baking tray in the last 3-4 mins to crisp up, then remove and set aside.

STEP 2

Scrape the vegetables into a pan, squeeze the garlic out of the skins, discarding the papery shells, and add with the stock, then blend with a stick blender until very smooth and creamy. Bring to a simmer and season with salt, pepper and nutmeg.

STEP 3

Divide between bowls. Serve with a swirl of yogurt and the crispy sage leaves.

SWEDISH MEATBALLS

Prep: 10 mins - Cook: 25 mins plus cooling and chilling - Serves 4

INGREDIENTS

- 2 tbsp rapeseed oil
- 1 onion , finely chopped
- 1 small garlic clove , finely grated
- 375g lean pork mince
- 1 medium egg yolk
- grating of nutmeg
- 50g fine fresh breadcrumbs
- 300ml hot low-salt beef stock

- ½ tbsp Dijon mustard

- 2 tbsp fat-free natural yogurt

- 400g spring greens , shredded

- lingonberry or cranberry sauce , to serve

DIRECTIONS

STEP 1

Put 1 tbsp rapeseed oil in a frying pan over a medium heat. Add the onion and fry for 10 mins or until soft and translucent. Add the garlic and cook for 1 min. Leave to cool.

STEP 2

Mix the cooled onions, pork mince, egg yolk, a good grating of nutmeg and the breadcrumbs in a bowl with your hands until well combined. Form into 12 balls and chill for 15 mins.

STEP 3

Heat the remaining oil in a frying pan and fry the meatballs for 5 mins over a medium heat, turning often until golden. Pour over the stock and bubble for 8-10 mins or until it has reduced a little. Stir through the mustard and yogurt.

STEP 4

Steam the greens for 5 mins or until tender. Serve the meatballs with the greens and a dollop of the sauce.

SINGAPORE NOODLES WITH PRAWNS

Prep: 10 mins - Cook: 10 mins - Serves 2

INGREDIENTS

- 2 nests thin vermicelli rice noodles

- 1 tbsp light soy sauce

- 1 tbsp oyster sauce

- 2 tsp mild curry powder

- 1 tbsp sesame oil

- 1 garlic clove , chopped

- 1 red chilli , thinly sliced (deseeded if you don't like it too hot)

- thumb-sized piece ginger , grated

- 1 medium onion , sliced

- 1 red pepper or yellow pepper, cut into thin batons

- 4 spring onions , cut in half lengthways then into batons

- 8 raw king prawns

- 1 large egg , beaten

- coriander leaves, to serve

DIRECTIONS

STEP 1

Soak the rice noodles in warm water for 5 mins until softened but still al dente. Drain and set aside.

STEP 2

In a small bowl, mix together the soy, oyster sauce and curry powder.

STEP 3

In a large wok, add half the oil and fry the garlic, chilli and ginger until golden, about 2 mins. Add the remaining oil, onion, pepper, spring onions, prawns and noodles and stir-fry for a few mins. Push everything to one side, add the egg and scramble. Add the soy sauce mixture, toss again for a few more mins, then remove from the heat. Sprinkle over the coriander leaves before serving.

SPICED CARROT & LENTIL SOUP

Prep: 10 mins   Cook: 15 mins - Serves 4

INGREDIENTS

- 2 tsp cumin seeds
- pinch chilli flakes
- 2 tbsp olive oil
- 600g carrots, washed and coarsely grated (no need to peel)
- 140g split red lentils
- 1l hot vegetable stock (from a cube is fine)
- 125ml milk (to make it dairy-free, see 'try' below)
- plain yogurt and naan bread, to serve

DIRECTIONS

STEP 1

Heat a large saucepan and dry-fry 2 tsp cumin seeds and a pinch of chilli flakes for 1 min, or until they start to jump around the pan and release their aromas.

STEP 2

Scoop out about half with a spoon and set aside. Add 2 tbsp olive oil, 600g coarsely grated carrots, 140g split red lentils, 1l hot vegetable stock and 125ml milk to the pan and bring to the boil.

STEP 3

Simmer for 15 mins until the lentils have swollen and softened.

STEP 4

Whizz the soup with a stick blender or in a food processor until smooth (or leave it chunky if you prefer).

STEP 5

Season to taste and finish with a dollop of plain yogurt and a sprinkling of the reserved toasted spices. Serve with warmed naan breads.

CHANA MASALA WITH POMEGRANATE RAITA

Prep: 10 mins - Cook: 35 mins - Serves 2

INGREDIENTS

- 1 tbsp rapeseed oil
- 2 onions , halved and thinly sliced
- 1 tbsp chopped ginger
- 2 large garlic cloves , finely grated or crushed
- 1 green chilli , halved, deseeded and thinly sliced
- ½ tsp cumin seeds
- ½ tsp mustard seeds
- ½ tsp garam masala
- ½ tsp turmeric
- 1 tsp ground coriander
- 400g can chickpeas , undrained
- 4 small tomatoes (about 160g), cut into wedges
- 2 tsp vegetable bouillon powder
- cooked wholegrain rice , to serve (optional)

For the pomegranate raita

- 150ml plain bio yogurt
- 25g pomegranate seeds
- 2 tbsp finely chopped coriander , plus extra leaves to serve

DIRECTIONS

STEP 1

Heat the oil in a large non-stick pan, then cook the onions, ginger, garlic and chilli for 15-20 mins.

STEP 2

Add the spices, chickpeas, the liquid from the can, ¾ can cold water, the tomatoes and bouillon. Cover and simmer for 10 mins.

STEP 3

Meanwhile, mix the ingredients for the raita in a small bowl, reserving a few coriander leaves. Roughly mash some of the curry to thicken it. Spoon into bowls with rice, if you like. Scatter over the reserved coriander and serve with the raita on the side.

LEEK, PEA & WATERCRESS SOUP

Prep: 10 mins - Cook: 22 mins - Serves 4

INGREDIENTS

- 1 tbsp olive oil , plus a drizzle to serve
- 2 leeks , finely sliced
- 4 small garlic cloves , crushed
- 650-800ml hot veg stock
- 80g watercress
- 400g frozen peas
- 1 small lemon , zested and juiced
- small bunch of parsley , finely chopped
- dairy-free crème fraîche and crusty bread, to serve (optional)

DIRECTIONS

STEP 1

Heat the oil in a large saucepan over a medium heat. Add the leeks and garlic and fry for 7-10 mins or until softened and translucent.

STEP 2

Pour in the hot stock and simmer for 5-10 mins. Stir through the watercress, reserving a few leaves for garnish, then the peas, and cook for 5 mins until wilted. Use a hand blender or processor and whizz until smooth. Stir through the lemon juice and zest, then season to taste. Stir through half the parsley. Ladle into bowls and top with the remaining parsley, reserved watercress and a drizzle of olive oil. Swirl through some crème fraîche, then serve with crusty bread, if you like.

COD WITH CUCUMBER, AVOCADO & MANGO SALSA SALAD

Prep: 5 mins - Cook: 8 mins - Serves 2

INGREDIENTS

- 2 x skinless cod fillets
- 1 lime , zested and juiced

- 1 small mango , peeled, stoned and chopped (or 2 peaches, stoned and chopped)
- 1 small avocado , stoned, peeled and sliced
- ¼ cucumber , chopped
- 160g cherry tomatoes , quartered
- 1 red chilli , deseeded and chopped
- 2 spring onions , sliced
- handful chopped coriander

DIRECTIONS

STEP 1

Heat oven to 200C/180C fan/gas 6. Put the fish in a shallow ovenproof dish and pour over half the lime juice, with a little of the zest, then grind over some black pepper. Bake for 8 mins or until the fish flakes easily but is still moist.

STEP 2

Meanwhile, put the rest of the ingredients, plus the remaining lime juice and zest, in a bowl and combine well. Spoon onto plates and top with the cod, spooning over any juices in the dish.

PRAWN FRIED RICE

Prep: 5 mins - Cook: 25 mins - Serves 4

INGREDIENTS

- 250g long-grain brown rice
- 150g frozen peas
- 100g mangetout
- 1½ tbsp rapeseed oil
- 1 onion , finely chopped
- 2 garlic cloves , crushed
- thumb-sized piece of ginger , finely grated
- 150g raw king prawns
- 3 medium eggs , beaten
- 2 tsp sesame seeds
- 1 tbsp low-salt soy sauce
- ½ tbsp rice or white wine vinegar
- 4 spring onions , trimmed and sliced

DIRECTIONS

STEP 1

Cook the rice following pack instructions. Boil a separate pan of water and blanch the peas and mangetout for 1 min, then drain and set aside with the rice.

STEP 2

Meanwhile, heat the oil in a large non-stick frying pan or wok over a medium heat and fry the onion for 10 mins or until golden brown. Add the garlic and ginger and fry for a further minute. Tip in the blanched vegetables and fry for 5 mins, then the prawns and fry for a further 2 mins. Stir the rice into the pan then push everything to one side. Pour the beaten eggs into the empty side of the pan and stir to scramble them. Fold everything together with the sesame seeds, soy and vinegar, then finish with the spring onions scattered over.

CHAKALAKA (SOWETO CHILLI)

Prep: 40 mins - Cook: 30 mins - Serves 6 - 8

INGREDIENTS

- 3 tbsp light olive oil , or vegetable oil
- 1 red or white onion , finely chopped
- 6 garlic cloves , crushed
- 1-2 green chillies , deseeded and chopped
- thumb-sized piece ginger , finely grated
- 2 tbsp milk, medium or hot curry powder
- 3 peppers (mix of red, green and yellow), finely chopped
- 5-6 large carrots , grated
- 2 tbsp tomato purée
- 5-6 large tomatoes or 400g can chopped tomatoes
- 2 tsp piri-piri spice blend
- 2 thyme sprigs , leaves only, or 2 tsp dried thyme
- spiced apple chutney , BBQ sauce, jerk sauce or piri-piri sauce to taste (optional)
- 400g can baked beans

To serve

- chopped coriander
- rice or mealie bread (South African cornbread)
- mixed green salad
- grilled meats

DIRECTIONS

STEP 1

Heat the oil in a casserole dish set over a medium heat. Add the onion and cook until soft and starting to caramelise.

STEP 2

Stir in the garlic, chillies and half the ginger. Cook for 1-2 mins, then add the curry powder and stir to make a curry paste. If the mixture is starting to catch, add a splash of water to stop it burning.

STEP 3

Stir in the peppers and cook for 2 mins more. Add the carrots and stir to make sure they are coated in the curry paste. Stir in the purée, tomatoes, piri-piri spice, thyme and apple chutney or sauce, if using.

STEP 4

Add the baked beans, then half-fill the can with water and add that too. Bring to the boil, reduce the heat and simmer for at least 10 mins until the vegetables are tender and the mixture has thickened.

STEP 5

Add the remaining ginger and season to taste. Sprinkle with coriander and serve hot or cold with rice or mealie bread, salad and grilled meats.

OMELETTE PANCAKES WITH TOMATO & PEPPER SAUCE

Prep: 10 mins - Cook: 20 mins - Serves 2

INGREDIENTS

- 4 large eggs
- handful basil leaves

For the sauce

- 2 tsp rapeseed oil , plus a little extra for the pancakes
- 1 yellow pepper , quartered, deseeded and thinly sliced
- 2 garlic cloves , thinly sliced
- 1 tbsp cider vinegar
- 400g can chopped tomatoes
- wholemeal bread or salad leaves, to serve

DIRECTIONS

STEP 1

First make the sauce. Heat the oil in a large frying pan, and fry the pepper and garlic for 5 mins to soften them. Spoon in the cider vinegar and allow to sizzle away. Tip in the tomatoes, then measure in a third of a can of water. Cover and leave to simmer for 10-15 mins until the peppers are tender and the sauce is thick.

STEP 2

Meanwhile, make the pancakes. Beat 1 egg with 1 tsp water and seasoning, then heat a small non-stick frying pan with a tiny amount of oil. Add the egg mixture and cook for 1-2 mins until set into a thin pancake. Lift onto a plate, cover with foil and repeat with the other eggs. Roll up onto warm plates, spoon over the sauce and scatter with the basil. Serve with bread or a salad on the side.

SPICY SPAGHETTI WITH GARLIC MUSHROOMS

Prep: 10 mins - Cook: 15 mins - Serves 4

INGREDIENTS

- 2 tbsp olive oil
- 250g pack chestnut mushroom, thickly sliced
- 1 garlic clove, thinly sliced
- small bunch parsley, leaves only
- 1 celery stick, finely chopped
- 1 onion, finely chopped
- 400g can chopped tomato
- 1/2 red chilli, deseeded and finely chopped, (or use drieds chilli flakes)
- 300g spaghetti

DIRECTIONS

STEP 1

Heat 1 tbsp oil in a pan, add the mushrooms, then fry over a high heat for 3 mins until golden and softened. Add the garlic, fry for 1 min more, then tip into a bowl with the parsley. Add the onion and celery to the pan with the rest of the oil, then fry for 5 mins until lightly coloured.

STEP 2

Stir in the tomatoes, chilli and a little salt, then bring to the boil. Reduce the heat and simmer, uncovered, for 10 mins until thickened. Meanwhile, boil the spaghetti, then drain. Toss with the sauce, top with the garlicky mushrooms, then serve.

TERIYAKI STEAK WITH PAK CHOI & NOODLES

Prep: 10 mins - Cook: 15 mins - Serves 2

INGREDIENTS

- ½ tsp Chinese five-spice powder
- 2 lean beef steak , 175g each
- 1 tbsp sunflower oil
- 2 pak choi , trimmed and quartered
- 1 medium carrot , thinly sliced
- 1 red pepper , deseeded and thinly sliced
- 150g pack straight-to-wok egg noodles
- 3 tbsp teriyaki sauce

DIRECTIONS

STEP 1

Mix the five-spice with 1/2 tsp flaky sea salt and 1/2 tsp black pepper, and rub into the steaks. Heat 1 tsp of the oil in a large, non-stick frying pan over a medium-high heat. Fry the steak for 4-5 mins each side or until done to your liking. Transfer to a warmed plate, cover loosely with foil and leave to rest.

STEP 2

Pour the remaining oil into the pan, add the pak choi, the carrot and pepper. Stir-fry for 3 mins, then add the noodles and stir-fry for 2 mins more.

STEP 3

Pour in the teriyaki sauce and simmer for a few secs, then divide the vegetable noodles between 2 warmed plates or shallow bowls. Slice the steak thickly and place on top.

SPEEDY MEDITERRANEAN GNOCCHI

Cook: 5 mins - Serves 2

INGREDIENTS

- 400g gnocchi
- 200g chargrilled vegetables (from the deli counter - I used chargrilled peppers, aubergines, artichokes and semi-dried tomatoes)
- 2 tbsp red pesto
- a handful of basil leaves
- parmesan or pecorino (or vegetarian alternative), to serve

DIRECTIONS

STEP 1

Boil a large pan of salted water. Add the gnocchi, cook for 2 mins or until it rises to the surface, then drain and tip back into the pan with a splash of reserved cooking water.

STEP 2

Add the chargrilled veg, chopped into pieces if large, red pesto and basil leaves. Serve with shavings of Parmesan or pecorino (or vegetarian alternative).

CHEAT'S CHICKEN RAMEN

Prep: 10 mins - Cook: 15 mins - 20 mins - Serves 4

INGREDIENTS

- 1.2l good-quality chicken stock
- small pack coriander, stalks and leaves separated
- 1 red chilli (deseeded if you don't like it too hot), sliced
- 2 tbsp light soy sauce
- 100g grey oyster mushrooms, sliced
- 100g pack baby pak choi
- 2 skinless cooked chicken breasts, sliced
- 100g egg noodles
- 50g sliced bamboo shoots

DIRECTIONS

STEP 1

Set a large saucepan over a medium heat and pour in the stock. Finely chop the coriander stalks and add to the stock with most of the chilli. Bring to the boil and add 200ml water. Once boiled, reduce the heat and simmer for 5-10 mins to infuse the coriander and chilli.

STEP 2

Add the soy sauce and a grinding of black pepper, then the mushrooms, pak choi, chicken and noodles. Simmer for 2 mins until the noodles soften, before adding the bamboo shoots.

STEP 3

Serve in deep bowls topped with coriander leaves and the remaining chilli slices.

MUSHROOM JACKET POTATOES

Prep: 10 mins - Cook: 1 hr and 25 mins - Serves 2

INGREDIENTS

- 2 large potatoes
- 2 tsp sunflower oil
- 250g mushrooms
- 100g sour cream & chive dip

- sprigs of dill (to garnish)

DIRECTIONS

STEP 1

Heat oven to 200C/180C fan/gas 6. Prick the potatoes all over with a fork and rub with half the sunflower oil. Bake the potatoes for 1 hr 20 mins.

STEP 2

Slice the mushrooms, fry in the remaining oil, then stir through half the sour cream & chive dip. Pile the mushrooms into the jacket potatoes and garnish with dill.

DHAL WITH GARAM MASALA CARROTS

Prep: 5 mins - Cook: 20 mins - Serves 1

INGREDIENTS

- 75g red lentils
- 1 garlic clove , peeled
- knob of salted butter
- 2 carrots , cut into batons
- 1 tbsp rapeseed oil
- ½ tsp garam masala
- 1 tsp nigella seeds (kalonji, optional)
- 1 tsp Greek yogurt

DIRECTIONS

STEP 1

Cook the lentils in 500ml water with the garlic clove for around 20 mins until the lentils are tender. Fish the garlic clove out, crush it and stir it back into the lentils with the butter. Season well. It should be spoonable like a thick soup – keep simmering if it's not thick enough.

STEP 2

Put the carrots in a pan, just cover with water, bring to the boil and simmer until just tender, about 8-10 mins. Drain, then toss in the oil and garam masala. Tip into a frying pan and fry until the carrots start to brown, then add the nigella seeds, if using, and fry for another min.

STEP 3

Serve the dhal in a bowl with the yogurt and carrots, with the remaining spices and oil from the pan on top.

SPICY TURKEY SWEET POTATOES

Prep: 5 mins - Cook: 45 mins - Serves 4

INGREDIENTS

- 4 sweet potatoes
- 1 tbsp olive oil
- 1 onion , finely chopped
- 1 garlic clove , crushed
- 500g pack turkey thigh mince
- 500g carton passata
- 3 tbsp barbecue sauce
- ½ tsp cayenne pepper
- 4 tbsp soured cream
- ½ pack chives , finely snipped

DIRECTIONS

STEP 1

Heat oven to 200C/180C fan/gas 6. Prick the potatoes, place on a baking tray and bake for 45 mins or until really soft.

STEP 2

Meanwhile, heat the oil in a frying pan, add the onion and cook gently for 8 mins until softened. Stir in the garlic, then tip in the mince and stir to break up. Cook over a high heat until any liquid has evaporated and the mince is browned, about 10 mins. Pour in the passata, then fill the carton a quarter full of water and tip that in too. Add the barbecue sauce and cayenne, then lower the heat and simmer gently for 15 mins, adding a little extra water if needed. Taste and season.

STEP 3

When the potatoes are soft, split them down the centre and spoon the mince over the top. Add a dollop of soured cream and a sprinkling of chives.

SINGAPORE CHILLI CRAB

Prep: 25 mins - Cook: 5 mins - Serves 2

INGREDIENTS

- 1 whole cooked crab (about 1kg)
- 2 tbsp flavourless oil
- 3 garlic cloves , very finely chopped
- thumb-sized piece ginger , very finely chopped
- 3 red chillies , 2 very finely chopped, 1 sliced
- 4 tbsp tomato ketchup

- 2 tbsp soy sauce
- handful coriander leaves, roughly chopped
- 2 spring onions , sliced
- rice or steamed bad buns, to serve

DIRECTIONS

STEP 1

The crab must be prepared before stir-frying (you can ask your fishmonger to do this). This involves removing the claws, the main shell, discarding the dead man's fingers, then cutting the body into four pieces, and cracking the claws and the legs so the sauce can get through to the meat.

STEP 2

Heat the oil in a large wok and sizzle the garlic, ginger and chopped chillies for 1 min or until fragrant. Add the ketchup, soy and 100ml water, and stir to combine. Throw in the crab, turn up the heat and stir-fry for 3-5 mins or until the crab is piping hot and coated in the sauce. Stir through most of the coriander, spring onions and sliced chilli.

STEP 3

Use tongs to arrange the crab on a serving dish, pour over the sauce from the pan and scatter over the remaining coriander, spring onions and sliced chilli. Serve with rice or bao buns, and a lot of napkins.

BAKED FALAFEL & CAULIFLOWER TABBOULEH

Prep: 30 mins - Cook: 20 mins - Serves 6

INGREDIENTS

- 3 x 400g cans chickpeas , drained (or 250g dried chickpeas, soaked in 1 litre cold water overnight, then drained)
- 3 tsp ground cumin
- 2 tsp ground coriander
- 1 tsp cayenne pepper
- 1 red onion , quartered
- 3 garlic cloves
- 2 tbsp sesame seeds
- 1 ½ tsp baking powder (gluten-free, if you like)
- 2 small packs parsley , stalks and leaves separated, leaves chopped
- 4 tbsp olive oil

- 1 cauliflower , cut into large florets
- 1 small pack mint , leaves chopped and stalks discarded
- 1 lemon , juiced

DIRECTIONS

STEP 1

Heat oven to 200C/180C fan/gas 6 and line two baking sheets with baking parchment. Tip the chickpeas, 2 tsp of the ground cumin, 1 tsp of the ground coriander, the cayenne pepper, onion, garlic, sesame seeds, baking powder, parsley stalks and 1 tbsp water into a food processor. Blitz until combined but not smooth (you want the falafel to have some texture, rather than being the consistency of hummus). Season to taste, then roll into 18 evenly sized balls. Flatten each ball into a disc shape and arrange on the baking sheets, then brush the tops with 1 tbsp of the oil. Bake for 20 mins until golden and crisp, turning halfway through cooking.

STEP 2

Meanwhile, clean out the food processor, then tip in the cauliflower and briefly pulse until it resembles couscous. Mix the cauliflower couscous with the remaining ground spices and olive oil, then add some seasoning. Tip onto a roasting tray and roast for 10-12 mins until lightly toasted, stirring occasionally.

STEP 3

Remove from the oven and leave to cool, then mix through the parsley leaves, mint leaves and lemon juice. Season to taste. Will keep for three days in the fridge. Serve the baked falafel with the cauliflower tabbouleh and some salad, if you like.

LENTIL FRITTERS

Prep: 15 mins - Cook: 10 mins - Serves 2

INGREDIENTS

- 300g leftover basic lentils
- handful of chopped coriander
- 1 chopped spring onion
- 50g gram flour
- 2 carrots
- 2 courgettes
- ½ tsp sesame seeds
- handful of coriander
- ½ tsp sesame oil
- juice of 1 lime

- 1 tbsp rapeseed oil

DIRECTIONS

STEP 1

Mix the leftover lentils with the chopped coriander, spring onion and gram flour, then set aside. Use a peeler to cut the carrots and courgettes into long ribbons, then toss the ribbons with the sesame seeds and coriander in sesame oil and the lime juice.

STEP 2

Heat the rapeseed oil in a frying pan. Spoon in four dollops of the lentil mixture and flatten into patties. Fry each side until golden and serve with the ribbon salad.

LAYERED AUBERGINE & LENTIL BAKE

Prep: 15 mins - Cook: 45 mins - Serves 4

INGREDIENTS

- 2 aubergines , cut into 0.5cm slices lengthways
- 3 tbsp olive oil
- 140g puy lentils
- 2 onions , finely chopped
- 3 garlic cloves , finely chopped
- 300g cooked butternut squash
- 400g can chopped tomato
- ½ small pack basil leaves
- 125g ball of mozzarella , torn

DIRECTIONS

STEP 1

Heat oven to 220C/200C fan/gas 7. Brush both sides of the aubergine slices with 2 tbsp of the oil, lay on baking sheets, season and bake for 15-20 mins until tender, turning once. Cook the lentils following pack instructions.

STEP 2

Heat the remaining oil in a large frying pan. Tip in the onions and garlic and cook until soft. Stir though the squash and the tomatoes, plus ½ can of water. Simmer for 10-15 mins until the sauce has thickened. Stir in the lentils, basil and seasoning.

STEP 3

Spoon a layer of lentils into a small baking dish. Top with aubergine slices and repeat, finishing with a layer of aubergine. Scatter with mozzarella and bake for a further 15 mins until the cheese is golden and bubbling.

STIR-FRIED PORK WITH GINGER & HONEY

Prep: 15 mins - Cook: 10 mins - Serves 2

INGREDIENTS

- 2 nests medium egg noodles
- 2 tsp cornflour
- 2 tbsp soy sauce
- 1 tbsp honey
- 1 tbsp sunflower oil
- 250g/9oz pork tenderloin, cut into bite-sized pieces
- thumb-sized piece ginger, finely chopped
- 2 garlic cloves, finely chopped
- 1 green pepper, deseeded and sliced
- 100g mange tout
- 1 tsp sesame seed

DIRECTIONS

STEP 1

Bring a pan of salted water to the boil and cook the noodles following pack instructions. Meanwhile, mix the cornflour with 1 tbsp water, then stir in the soy sauce and honey, and set aside.

STEP 2

Heat the oil in a wok over a high heat. Add the pork and cook for 2 mins until browned all over. Add the ginger, garlic, pepper and mangetout, and cook for a further 2 mins. Reduce the heat, then add the soy and honey mixture, stirring and cooking until the sauce bubbles and thickens. Divide the drained noodles between 2 bowls. Top with the pork and vegetables, and finish with a sprinkling of sesame seeds.

EASY PULLED BEEF RAGU

Prep: 20 mins - Cook: 4 hrs - 8 (or 2 meals for 4)

INGREDIENTS

- 2 tbsp olive oil
- 1kg boneless beef brisket
- 2 onions , finely chopped
- 4 garlic cloves , finely chopped

* 5 carrots , thickly sliced

* 250ml red wine

* 2 x 400g cans chopped tomatoes

* 2 tbsp tomato purée

* 4 bay leaves

* 450g large pasta shapes (such as paccheri, rigate or rigatoni)

* large handful basil leaves , to serve

* grated parmesan , to serve

DIRECTIONS

STEP 1

Heat oven to 150C/130C fan/gas 2. Heat 1 tbsp oil in a flameproof casserole dish and brown the beef all over. Take the beef out of the dish, add the remaining oil and gently cook the onions and garlic for 10 mins until softened.

STEP 2

Add the browned beef back to the dish with the carrots, red wine, tomatoes, tomato purée and bay leaves. Cover with foil and a lid, and slowly cook for 3 - 3 1/2 hrs or until the meat falls apart. Check on it a couple of times, turning the beef over and giving it a good stir to make sure it's coated in the sauce.

STEP 3

Cook the pasta following pack instructions, then drain. Shred the beef – it should just fall apart when you touch it with a fork – then spoon the beef and tomato sauce over the pasta. Scatter with basil and Parmesan before serving.

ALMOND CRÊPES WITH AVOCADO & NECTARINES

Prep: 10 mins - Cook: 5 mins - Serves 2

INGREDIENTS

* 2 large eggs

* 3 tbsp ground almonds

* 2 tsp rapeseed oil

* 1 avocado , halved, stoned and flesh lightly crushed

* 2 ripe nectarines , stoned and sliced

* seeds from 1/2 pomegranate

* ½ lime , cut into 2 wedges, for squeezing over

DIRECTIONS

STEP 1

Beat one egg and 1 1 /2 tbsp of the almonds in a small bowl with 1 tbsp water. Heat 1 tsp oil in a large non-stick frying pan over a medium heat and pour in the egg mixture, swirling the pan to evenly cover the base. Cook until the mixture sets and turns golden on the underside, about 2 mins. (There is no need to flip it over.) Turn it out onto a plate and make another one with 1 tbsp water, the remaining egg, oil and almonds.

STEP 2

Top each crêpe with the avocado, nectarines and pomegranate, and squeeze over the lime at the table.

SKINNY LAMB BIRYANI

Prep: 15 mins - Cook: 20 mins - Serves 2

INGREDIENTS

For the cauliflower pilau

- 350g cauliflower florets
- ½ tsp turmeric
- 3 cardamom pods , lightly crushed
- ½ tsp fennel seeds , lightly crushed
- a few pinches of black onion seeds or nigella seeds

For the spicy lamb

- 1 tbsp rapeseed oil
- 1 large onion , finely chopped
- 1 tbsp finely chopped ginger
- 1 red chilli , deseeded and finely chopped
- 2 garlic cloves , thinly sliced
- 1 tsp ground cumin
- 1 tsp ground coriander
- 200g very lean lamb steak, cut into bite-sized pieces
- 200g can chopped tomatoes
- 1 tsp bouillon
- 15g toasted flaked almonds
- 50g pomegranate seeds
- handful small mint leaves

DIRECTIONS

STEP 1

Put the cauliflower in a food processor and pulse until it is reduced to rice-sized pieces. Tip into a large bowl and stir in the turmeric, cardamom, fennel seeds, black onion seeds and some seasoning. Cover with cling film, pierce and set aside.

STEP 2

For the spicy lamb, heat the oil in a non-stick wok and fry the onion and ginger for 10 mins until soft and golden. Add the chilli and garlic, and cook for 1 min more.

STEP 3

Stir in the cumin and coriander, cook briefly, then toss in the lamb and stir-fry for 1-2 mins until pale brown. Add the tomatoes and the bouillon, and cook for 2 mins - you are aiming for a thick sauce and really tender lamb that is still a little pink and juicy.

STEP 4

Meanwhile, put the cauliflower in the microwave and cook on high for 3 mins. Tip out onto serving plates, dot the lamb and sauce in patches over the rice, then scatter with the almonds, pomegranate seeds and mint leaves to serve.

LIGHTER SPAGHETTI & MEATBALLS

Prep: 30 mins - Cook: 35 mins - Serves 4

INGREDIENTS

- 1 tsp rapeseed oil
- 280g spaghetti

For the meatballs

- 200g green lentils (well drained weight from a 400g can)
- 250g lean minced pork (max 8% fat)
- ½ tsp finely chopped rosemary
- ½ tsp Dijon mustard
- 1 garlic clove , crushed

For the sauce

- 1 tbsp rapeseed oil
- 2 shallots , finely chopped
- 2 garlic cloves , finely chopped
- 500g cherry tomatoes , preferably on the vine, halved
- 2 tsp tomato purée
- pinch of chilli flakes
- 2 tbsp chopped oregano , plus a few chopped leaves to garnish

DIRECTIONS

STEP 1

Heat oven to 200C/180C fan/gas 6. Line a baking sheet with foil and brush with 1 tsp oil. Mash the lentils in a bowl with the back of a fork to break down a bit, but not completely. Stir in the pork, rosemary, mustard, garlic, some pepper to generously season, and mix well with the fork to distribute the lentils evenly. Divide the mixture into 4. Form each quarter into 5 small balls – to give you 20 in total – squeezing the mixture together well as you shape it. Lay the meatballs on the foil and roll them around in the oil to coat all over. Bake for 15 mins until cooked and lightly browned. Remove (leave the oven on) and set aside.

STEP 2

While the meatballs cook, heat 2 tsp of the oil for the sauce in a large non-stick frying pan. Tip in the shallots and garlic, and fry on a medium heat for 3-4 mins until softened and tinged brown. Pour in the remaining 1 tsp oil, lay the tomatoes in the pan so most of them are cut-side down (to help release the juices), raise the heat and fry them for 3-4 mins or until the tomatoes are starting to soften and release their juices. Don't stir, or they may lose their shape. Splash in 125-150ml water so it all bubbles, and gently mix in the tomato purée. Lower the heat and simmer for 2 mins to create a juicy, chunky sauce. Season with the chilli flakes, oregano, pepper and a pinch of salt, and give it a quick stir, adding a drop more water if needed – you want it thick enough to coat the meatballs.

STEP 3

Pour the sauce into a casserole dish, add the meatballs and spoon the sauce over them to coat. Cover with foil and bake for 10 mins while you cook the spaghetti.

STEP 4

Boil a large saucepan of water. Add the spaghetti, stir and bring back to the boil. Cook for 10-12 mins, or following pack instructions, until al dente. Drain well, season with pepper and serve with the meatballs, sauce and a light sprinkling of oregano.

CHOCOLATE-ORANGE STEAMED PUDDING WITH CHOCOLATE SAUCE

Prep: 25 mins - Cook: 1 hr and 30 mins - Serves 8

INGREDIENTS

For the chocolate sauce

- 50g cocoa
- 50g butter , plus extra for greasing
- 100g Total Sweet (xylitol, see tip)

- 1 tsp vanilla extract
- 200ml semi-skimmed milk

For the pudding

- 1 small orange
- 100g Total Sweet (xylitol)
- 225g self-raising flour
- 50g cocoa
- 150ml semi-skimmed milk
- 1 tsp vanilla extract
- 2 large eggs

DIRECTIONS

STEP 1

First, make the sauce. Sift the cocoa into a small saucepan, add all the other ingredients, then warm over a medium-high heat, stirring. Allow to bubble hard for 1 min to make a glossy sauce. Spoon 4 tbsp into the base of a lightly buttered, traditional 1.2 litre pudding basin. Leave the rest to cool, stirring occasionally.

STEP 2

Put a very large pan (deep enough to enclose the whole pudding basin) of water on to boil with a small upturned plate placed in the base of the pan to support the basin.

STEP 3

Zest the orange, then cut the peel and pith away, and cut between the membrane to release the segments. Put all the pudding ingredients, except the orange segments, in a food processor and blitz until smooth. Add the orange segments and pulse to chop them into the pudding mixture. Spoon the mixture into the pudding basin, smoothing to the edges.

STEP 4

Tear off a sheet of foil and a sheet of baking parchment, both about 30cm long. Butter the baking parchment and use to cover the foil. Fold a 3cm pleat in the middle of the sheets, then place over the pudding, buttered baking parchment-side down. Tie with string under the lip of the basin, making a handle as you go. Trim the excess parchment and foil to about 5cm, then tuck the foil around the parchment to seal. Lower the basin into the pan of water, checking that the water comes two-thirds of the way up the sides of the basin, then cover the pan with a lid to trap the steam and simmer for 1 1/2 hours.

STEP 5

Carefully unwrap the pudding – it should now be risen and firm – and turn out of the basin on to a plate. Spoon over some warmed sauce and serve the rest separately with slices of the pudding.

BEAN & BARLEY SOUP

Prep: 5 mins - Cook: 1 hr - Serves 4

INGREDIENTS

- 2 tbsp vegetable oil
- 1 large onion , finely chopped
- 1 fennel bulb , quartered, cored and sliced
- 5 garlic cloves , crushed
- 400g can chickpea , drained and rinsed
- 2 x 400g cans chopped tomatoes
- 600ml vegetable stock
- 250g pearl barley
- 215g can butter beans , drained and rinsed
- 100g pack baby spinach leaves
- grated parmesan , to serve

DIRECTIONS

STEP 1

Heat the oil in a saucepan over a medium heat, add the onion, fennel and garlic, and cook until softened and just beginning to brown, about 10-12 mins.

STEP 2

Mash half the chickpeas and add to the pan with the tomatoes, stock and barley. Top up with a can of water and bring to the boil, then reduce the heat and simmer, covered, for 45 mins or until the barley is tender. Add another can of water if the liquid has significantly reduced.

STEP 3

Add the remaining chickpeas and the butter beans to the soup. After a few mins, stir in the spinach and cook until wilted, about 1 min. Season and serve scattered with Parmesan.

SUPER-QUICK SESAME RAMEN

Prep: 5 mins - Cook: 10 mins - Serves 1

INGREDIENTS

- 80g pack instant noodles (look for an Asian brand with a flavour like sesame)
- 2 spring onions , finely chopped
- ½ head pak choi
- 1 egg
- 1 tsp sesame seeds
- chilli sauce , to serve

DIRECTIONS

STEP 1

Cook the noodles with the sachet of flavouring provided (or use stock instead of the sachet, if you have it). Add the spring onions and pak choi for the final min.

STEP 2

Meanwhile, simmer the egg for 6 mins from boiling, run it under cold water to stop it cooking, then peel it. Toast the sesame seeds in a frying pan.

STEP 3

Tip the noodles and greens into a deep bowl, halve the boiled egg and place on top. Sprinkle with sesame seeds, then drizzle with the sauce or sesame oil provided with the noodles, and chilli sauce, if using.

SMOKY SPICED VEGGIE RICE

Prep: 15 mins - Cook: 1 hr - Serves 6

INGREDIENTS

- 25g cashews
- 4 tbsp olive oil
- 1 corn cob
- 250g rainbow baby carrots , halved lengthways
- 2 red onions , finely chopped
- 2 celery sticks , finely chopped
- 2 large red peppers , finely sliced
- 3 garlic cloves , crushed
- 2 tbsp Cajun seasoning
- 1½ tbsp smoked paprika
- 1 tsp chipotle paste
- 2 tbsp tomato purée
- 200g heirloom cherry tomatoes , halved
- 400g can kidney beans , drained and rinsed
- 400g can cherry tomatoes
- 300g long-grain rice , washed
- 400ml vegetable or vegan stock
- 1 tbsp red wine vinegar (vegan varieties are readily available)
- 2 tbsp caster sugar
- 2 spring onions , finely sliced

DIRECTIONS

STEP 1

Dry-fry the cashews in a large saucepan or casserole dish over a medium heat until golden brown. Remove from the heat, leave to cool, then roughly chop. Heat 1 tbsp oil in the same pan over a high heat, then fry the corn on each side for 20 seconds to char. Remove from the pan, set aside, then tip in the carrots and fry for 5 mins. Remove from the pan and set aside.

STEP 2

Heat the rest of the oil in the same pan over a medium heat and fry the onions and celery for 10 mins until soft and slightly coloured. Tip in the peppers and garlic, then fry for another 5 mins before adding the Cajun seasoning, smoked paprika, chipotle paste and tomato purée. Fry for 1 min until the spices are fragrant, then add the cherry tomatoes and fry for another 2 mins.

STEP 3

Stir in the kidney beans, canned tomatoes, rice, stock, vinegar and sugar, then stir until everything is combined. Bring to the boil, then cover with a lid and simmer with a lid on for 35-40 mins on a medium-low heat, stirring halfway through, until the rice is cooked and liquid absorbed.

STEP 4

Slice the corn off the cob and mix it through the rice along with the carrots. Season and garnish with the spring onions and cashews.

SPICED CHICKEN, SPINACH & SWEET POTATO STEW

Prep: 15 mins - Cook: 40 mins - Serves 4

INGREDIENTS

- 3 sweet potatoes, cut into chunks
- 190g bag spinach
- 1 tbsp sunflower oil
- 8 chicken thighs, skinless and boneless
- 500ml chicken stock

For the spice paste

- 2 onions, chopped
- 1 red chilli, chopped
- 1 tsp paprika
- thumb-sized piece ginger, grated

- 400g can tomatoes
- 2 preserved lemons, deseeded and chopped

To serve

- pumpkin seeds, toasted
- 2-3 preserved lemons, deseeded and chopped
- 4 naan bread, warmed

DIRECTIONS

STEP 1

Put the sweet potato in a large, deep saucepan over a high heat. Cover with boiling water and boil for 10 mins. Meanwhile, put all the paste ingredients in a food processor and blend until very finely chopped. Set aside until needed.

STEP 2

Put the spinach in a large colander in the sink and pour the sweet potatoes and their cooking water over it to drain the potatoes and wilt the spinach at the same time. Leave to steam-dry.

STEP 3

Return the saucepan to the heat (no need to wash it first), then add the oil, followed by the spice paste. Fry the paste for about 5 mins until thickened, then add the chicken. Fry for 8-10 mins until the chicken starts to colour. Pour over the stock, bring to the boil and leave to simmer for 10 mins, stirring occasionally.

STEP 4

Check the chicken is cooked by cutting into one of the thighs and making sure it's white throughout with no signs of pink. Season with black pepper, then add the sweet potato. Leave to simmer for a further 5 mins. Meanwhile, roughly chop the spinach and add to the stew. At this point you can leave the stew to cool and freeze for up to 3 months, if you like.

STEP 5

Scatter over the pumpkin seeds and preserved lemons, and serve with warm naan bread on the side.

PRAWN JAMBALAYA

Prep: 10 mins - Cook: 35 mins - Serves 2

INGREDIENTS

- 1 tbsp rapeseed oil
- 1 onion , chopped
- 3 celery sticks , sliced
- 100g wholegrain basmati rice
- 1 tsp mild chilli powder

- 1 tbsp ground coriander
- ½ tsp fennel seeds
- 400g can chopped tomatoes
- 1 tsp vegetable bouillon powder
- 1 yellow pepper , roughly chopped
- 2 garlic cloves , chopped
- 1 tbsp fresh thyme leaves
- 150g pack small prawns , thawed if frozen
- 3 tbsp chopped parsley

DIRECTIONS

STEP 1

Heat the oil in a large, deep frying pan. Add the onion and celery, and fry for 5 mins to soften. Add the rice and spices, and pour in the tomatoes with just under 1 can of water. Stir in the bouillon powder, pepper, garlic and thyme.

STEP 2

Cover the pan with a lid and simmer for 30 mins until the rice is tender and almost all the liquid has been absorbed

CHIVE WAFFLES WITH MAPLE & SOY MUSHROOMS

Prep: 25 mins - Cook: 20 mins - Serves 6

INGREDIENTS

- 500ml soya milk or rice milk
- 1 tsp cider vinegar or lemon juice
- 2 tbsp rapeseed oil
- 100g cooked, mashed sweet potato
- 150g polenta
- 130g plain flour
- 1 tbsp baking powder
- small bunch chives , snipped
- 1 tbsp maple syrup
- 2 tsp light soy sauce
- 6 large mushrooms , thickly sliced

- olive oil , for frying
- soya yogurt , to serve (optional)

DIRECTIONS

STEP 1

Heat the waffle iron. Mix the soya or rice milk with the vinegar and rapeseed oil (don't worry if it starts to split), then whisk in the sweet potato mash. Tip the polenta, flour and baking powder into a bowl, mix and make a well in the centre. Add a large pinch of salt, then slowly pour in the milk mixture and whisk to make a batter. Stir in half the chives.

STEP 2

Pour enough batter into the waffle iron to fill and cook for 4-5 mins. Lift out the waffle, keep it warm and repeat with the remaining mixture until you have six waffles.

STEP 3

Meanwhile, mix the maple syrup with the soy sauce. Brush it over the mushrooms and season with pepper. Heat a little oil in a frying pan and fry the mushrooms on both sides until they are browned and cooked through – make sure they don't burn at the edges. Serve the waffles topped with mushrooms, add a spoonful of soya yogurt, if you like, and scatter over the remaining chives.

SOUTH INDIAN COCONUT & PRAWN CURRY

Prep: 15 mins - Cook: 25 mins - 30 mins - Serves 2

INGREDIENTS

- 1 large onion , quartered
- 0.5 thumb-sized piece ginger (no need to peel)
- 4 garlic cloves
- 4 tomatoes , 2 halved, 2 cut into wedges
- 2 tsp rapeseed oil
- ½ cinnamon stick
- ½ tsp black mustard seeds
- 3 cloves
- seeds from 4 cardamom pods , crushed
- ½ tsp ground turmeric
- 1 tsp ground coriander
- 10 fresh or dried curry leaves

- ½ fish stock cube

- 15g creamed coconut , chopped

- 1 red chilli , halved, deseeded and sliced or diced

- 150g pack raw, shelled king prawns

- 140g skinless cod , cut in half, then halve again to make chunky strips

DIRECTIONS

STEP 1

Put the onion, ginger, garlic and the halved tomatoes in a food processor with 50ml water and blitz to a smooth purée. You may need to scrape down the inside of the food processor a couple of times. Heat the oil in a large, deep non-stick frying pan, pour in the purée, cover with a lid and cook for 10 mins.

STEP 2

Add the 1/2 cinnamon stick, mustard seeds, cloves, cardamom, turmeric, coriander and curry leaves, and cook for a few mins, stirring. Pour in 300ml water with the stock cube, coconut and chilli, then leave to simmer for 10 mins more. Taste to ensure that the onion is fully cooked – if not, it is worth cooking for another 5 mins.

STEP 3

Finally, add the tomato wedges, prawns and fish, gently stir into the sauce, then cover and cook for 5 mins. Serve with the Spicy cauliflower pilau (see Goes well with).

HARISSA TROUT, BEETROOT & GRAPEFRUIT SALAD WITH WHIPPED FETA

Prep: 20 mins - Cook: 45 mins - Serves 2

INGREDIENTS

- 300g raw beetroot , scrubbed, skin left on

- 30g feta

- 2 tbsp 0% fat natural yogurt

- 1 lemon , zested and juiced

- 2 tbsp quinoa (optional)

- 1 pink grapefruit

- 1 tbsp extra virgin olive oil

- 1 tbsp harissa

- 2 trout fillets

- 2 red chicory , separated into leaves

- ½ small pack dill , leaves picked

DIRECTIONS

STEP 1

Bring a saucepan of water to the boil. Season the water, drop in the beetroot and cover the pan with a lid. Cook for 30-45 mins, depending on their size, until a cutlery knife can be easily inserted into them.

STEP 2

Meanwhile, heat oven to 200C/180C fan/gas 6. Put the feta in a bowl and mash with a fork, then beat in the yogurt and season with the lemon juice and zest to taste. In a dry frying pan, toast the quinoa, if using, until it pops. Set both aside.

STEP 3

Segment the grapefruit over a bowl to catch the juices, squeezing out as much as possible. Put the segments to one side, then whisk the olive oil with the juice. Season to taste with lemon juice, salt and pepper. You want it to be really tangy, as all the acidity will be absorbed by the beets.

STEP 4

Rub the harissa over the trout, season, then roast in the oven for 8-10 mins until just cooked.

STEP 5

Drain the beetroot. Once cool enough to handle, peel off the skin – it should come away easily. Cut into segments, then put onto a salad plate along with the chicory leaves. Pour the dressing over the warm beets and toss together. Nestle in the grapefruit segments, trout, harissa and dill, then add dollops of the feta and scatter over the toasted quinoa, if using.

SQUASH & LENTIL SALAD

Prep: 10 mins - Cook: 35 mins - Serves 2

INGREDIENTS

- 350g chopped butternut squash

- 4 tbsp olive oil

- 75g cucumber & mint raita or tzatziki

- 250g pack puy lentils

- small bunch dill

DIRECTIONS

STEP 1

Heat oven to 220C/200C/gas 7. Toss the squash in 2 tbsp olive oil, season and roast for 30-35 mins or until golden.

STEP 2

Add 2-3 tsp water to the raita, stir until smooth and set aside. Toss the lentils with half the raita, squash and dill. Tip the lentils onto a plate, top with remaining squash, drizzle over 2 tsp olive oil and the rest of the raita. Garnish with the remaining dill.

MEDITERRANEAN TURKEY-STUFFED PEPPERS

Prep: 20 mins - Cook: 30 mins - Serves 2

INGREDIENTS

- 2 red peppers (about 220g)
- 1 ½ tbsp olive oil, plus an extra drizzle
- 240g lean turkey breast mince (under 8% fat)
- ½ small onion, chopped
- 1 garlic clove, grated
- 1 tsp ground cumin
- 3-4 mushrooms, sliced
- 400g can chopped tomatoes
- 1 tbsp tomato purée
- 1 chicken stock cube
- handful fresh oregano leaves
- 60g mozzarella, grated
- 150g green vegetables (spinach, kale, broccoli, mangetout or green beans), to serve

DIRECTIONS

STEP 1

Heat oven to 190C/170C fan/gas 5. Halve the peppers lengthways, then remove the seeds and core but keep the stalks on. Rub the peppers with a drizzle of olive oil and season well. Put on a baking tray and roast for 15 mins.

STEP 2

Meanwhile, heat 1 tbsp olive oil in a large pan over a medium heat. Fry the mince for 2-3 mins, stirring to break up the chunks, then tip onto a plate.

STEP 3

Wipe out your pan, then heat the rest of the oil over a medium-high heat. Add the onion and garlic, stir-fry for 2-3 mins, then add the cumin and mushrooms and cook for 2-3 mins more.

STEP 4

Tip the mince back into the pan and add the chopped tomatoes and tomato purée. Crumble in the stock cube and cook for 3-4 mins, then add the oregano and season. Remove the peppers from the oven and fill them with as much of the mince as you can. (Don't worry if some spills out it – it will go satisfyingly crisp in the oven.) Top with the cheese and return to the oven for 10-15 mins until the cheese starts to turn golden.

STEP 5

Carefully slide the peppers onto a plate and serve alongside a pile of your favourite greens blanched, boiled or steamed.

MANGO SORBET

Prep: 15 mins plus freezing - Serves 8

INGREDIENTS

- 3 large, ripe mangoes
- 200g caster sugar
- 1 lime , juiced

DIRECTIONS

STEP 1

Peel the mangoes with a vegetable peeler, cut as much of the flesh away from the stone as you can, put it in a food processor or blender.

STEP 2

Add the sugar, lime juice and 200ml water. Blend for a few minutes, until the mango is very smooth and the sugar has dissolved – rub a little of the mixture between your fingers, if it still feels gritty, blend for a little longer. Pour into a container and put in the freezer for a few hours.

STEP 3

Scrape the sorbet back into the blender (if it's very solid, leave at room temperature for 5-10 mins first). Whizz until you have a slushy mixture, then pour back into the tin and freeze for another hour or so.

STEP 4

Repeat **step 3**. Freeze until solid (another hour or two). Will keep covered in the freezer for three months.

CREAMY TOMATO SOUP

Prep: 30 mins - Cook: 45 mins - Serves 6 adults and 6 kids

INGREDIENTS

- 3 tbsp olive oil
- 2 onions, chopped
- 2 celery sticks, chopped
- 300g carrot, chopped
- 500g potato, diced
- 4 bay leaves
- 5 tbsp tomato purée
- 2 tbsp sugar
- 2 tbsp red or white wine vinegar
- 4 x 400g cans chopped tomatoes
- 500g passata
- 3 vegetable stock cubes
- 400ml whole milk

DIRECTIONS

STEP 1

Put the oil, onions, celery, carrots, potatoes and bay leaves in a big casserole dish, or two saucepans. Fry gently until the onions are softened – about 10-15 mins. Fill the kettle and boil it.

STEP 2

Stir in the tomato purée, sugar, vinegar, chopped tomatoes and passata, then crumble in the stock cubes. Add 1 litre boiling water and bring to a simmer. Cover and simmer for 15 mins until the potato is tender, then remove the bay leaves. Purée with a stick blender (or ladle into a blender in batches) until very smooth. Season to taste and add a pinch more sugar if it needs it. The soup can now be cooled and chilled for up to 2 days, or frozen for up to 3 months.

STEP 3

To serve, reheat the soup, stirring in the milk – try not to let it boil. Serve in small bowls for the children with cheesy sausage rolls then later in bowls for the adults as Hot Bloody Mary soup (see 'Goes well with' recipes, below).